324.2736 Sanders, Arthur B.
San
          Victory.

DATE			

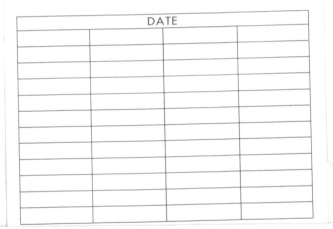

AMERICAN POLITICAL INSTITUTIONS AND PUBLIC POLICY

Stephen J. Wayne
Series Editor

VICTORY
How a Progressive Democratic Party Can Win and Govern
Arthur Sanders

THE POLITICS OF JUSTICE
The Attorney General and the Making of Legal Policy
Cornell W. Clayton

AMERICAN POLITICAL INSTITUTIONS AND PUBLIC POLICY

VICTORY

How a Progressive Democratic Party Can Win and Govern

ARTHUR SANDERS

M.E. Sharpe Inc.
Armonk, New York • London, England

Library of Congress Cataloging-in-Publication Data

Sanders, Arthur B.
Victory: how a progressive Democratic Party can win and govern/
by Arthur Sanders.
p.   cm
— (American political institutions and public policy)
Includes bibliographical references and index.
ISBN 1-56324-087-4 (cloth)
ISBN 1-56324-088-2 (pbk.)
1. Democratic Party (U.S.)—Platforms.
2. United States—Politics and government—1989–
I. Title.
II. Series.
JK2316.S25   1992
324.2736—dc20
92-13465
CIP

Printed in the United States of America

The paper used in this publication meets the minimum requirements of
American National Standard for Information Sciences—
Permanence of Paper for Printed Library Materials,
ANSI Z39.48–1984.

∞

MV(c)   10   9   8   7   6   5   4   3   2   1
MV(p)   10   9   8   7   6   5   4   3   2

For Deborah,
and for Ben.

Contents

PART THREE: BUILDING A PROGRESSIVE DEMOCRATIC PARTY

List of Tables

Foreword

Arthur Sanders, a professor of political science at Drake University, is a bridge builder. In this book he connects two divergent and often belligerent camps; that of the academician and that of the practitioner. Sanders is concerned with both democratic theory and the Democratic Party. He is interested in representation and responsiveness on the one hand, and the Democrats' winning national elections and governing effectively on the other. What he does in *Victory* is argue that both of these objectives can be achieved, that the Democratic Party should be more sensitive to its core constituency and that by so doing it can both win and govern.

The case Sanders makes for a progressive Democratic Party confounds conventional wisdom. It rejects the interpretation of most political pundits that Democratic candidates need to move to the center if they are to win presidential elections, an interpretation that the party's recent nominees seem to have accepted.

To make his case, Sanders dons his professorial cap as a political scientist. He presents and analyzes data on public opinion and voting behavior to support his claim that there is a sufficiently large population and voter base that would be energized by a progressive appeal. And this energy not only would increase the Democratic vote; it would rejuvenate the entire political system. Given the low voter turnout and the high levels of cynicism and apathy that plague the contemporary electorate, that would be no small accomplishment.

Obviously identifying a potential vote is not the same thing as obtaining it. Sanders addresses the "how to do it" issue as well by discussing the type of appeal the Demcorats should make and the general category of issues they should stress. He believes that the Democrats can rebuild their majority coalition, can win in the Electoral College, and can provide responsible party government. Thus, what he presents is an argument for action and a blueprint for victory. His is a compelling case, written with flare and without social science jargon but predicated on social science data, a case which party leaders will have to consider seriously in the 1990s. Let the debate over the composition and disposition of the Democratic Party begin once again!

Stephen J. Wayne
Georgetown University

Acknowledgments

One of the pleasures of writing a book about the future of the Democratic Party and American politics is that you are always "doing research." Dinner conversations, classroom discussions, lunchtime chats all serve as forums to try out ideas and engage in dialogue about the topics contained in these pages. I, thus, owe an enormous debt of gratitude to the many friends, colleagues, and students who have discussed and argued with me about the future of American politics and the Democratic Party over the years. In particular, my thinking about these matters has profited greatly from my conversations with Jim White of the Congressional Budget Office, Vin Auger of the Hamilton College Department of Government, Ken Wagner, director of The Swedish Program, Deborah Gerner and Phil Schrodt of Kansas University, and two of my colleagues here at Drake University, David Skidmore and Dennis Goldford. Their friendly encouragement, spirited debate, and general insights have helped to guide my thinking about these matters. Dennis, in addition, took the time to read a draft of the manuscript and his comments were quite helpful.

Some of the ideas contained in this book were also presented at a panel run by the "Political Scientists for a Progressive Democratic Party" at the 1991 Meeting of the Midwest Political Science Association. The comments and suggestions made by the other panelists, James MacGregor Burns of Williams College, Andrew Dobelstein of the University of North Carolina, Gary

Orfield of Chicago University, Monica Bauer of Western New England College, and especially the two discussants, Lois Lovelace Duke of Clemson University and Sue Thomas of Georgetown University, were quite useful, as were the detailed comments sent to me after that panel by Vernon Van Dyke of the University of Iowa. In addition, two anonymous reviewers of the manuscript provided valuable and useful criticism and commentary.

I also want to pay a special thanks to the students in my classes on American politics, particularly those in my classes on "The American Electoral Process" and "Political Parties and Interest Groups." Over the years they have listened to, challenged, and discussed many of the ideas contained in this book. It would be impossible to list all of the fine students I have had in these classes, but I want to make special note of one, Mark Elias. Mark was the kind of student who makes teaching a pleasure. He was always thinking, questioning, and challenging. If class ended and he was still not satisfied, he would come by to pick up the argument later. I know when we discussed the future of the Democratic Party he did not think he was helping me write a book, but he was.

Michael Weber of M.E. Sharpe, Inc. also deserves thanks. He has been encouraging, helpful, and easy to work with.

Finally, my family. A special thanks to my wife, Deborah Pappenheimer. She has contributed to this project in more ways than she knows. Our conversations about politics are always interesting and often spirited. Her love and support encouraged me to put my ideas into a manuscript. And our life together provides me with the love, peace, and security I need. Our three-year-old, Ben Pappenheimer, is too young to understand the ideas presented in this book, but as he learns to share and play with others, he is already developing a sense of justice and fairness that give me hope for a more just and progressive society. And the demands and needs of a three-year-old also help keep life in perspective. He does not really care if I want to read one more article in the paper. He wants to play with dad. My family gives me much more than I could ever give them, and I have dedicated this book to them.

VICTORY

1

Introduction

On November 8, 1988 George Bush resoundingly defeated Michael Dukakis to win election as the forty-first President of the United States. It was the fifth time in six elections that a Republican President had been elected, and the Democratic Party was once again faced with the dilemma of what to do to regain the Presidency. The year had seemed to be a promising one for the Democrats. Vice-President Bush appeared to be a vulnerable candidate. No sitting Vice-President had been elected to the Presidency since Martin Van Buren. The final years of the Reagan Presidency had been marked by scandal, and there was public concern about the future. Furthermore, the Democrats seemed to come out of their convention more united than they had been since 1964. But by election day, all of that seemed like wishful thinking.

For many, the lesson of 1988 was that a northeastern Democratic liberal could not be elected President. George Bush had continually attacked Governor Dukakis as a "liberal," and these attacks seemed to be effective. The Bush victory, coming on the heels of two terms of Ronald Reagan, seemed to indicate that the nation did, indeed, prefer conservative Republican leadership. Many urged the Democrats to "move to the center."

Michael Dukakis, however, did not lose the Presidency because he was too liberal. He lost because he did not clearly articulate a progressive vision. When he announced at the convention that the 1988 election was "not about ideology but about competence," he signaled his defeat. If the Democrats are not going to offer an alternative agenda and ideology, why should the public support them? If the Republican agenda is America's political agenda, surely the public is sensible in voting for a Repub-

3

lican to lead us in implementing that agenda. Electing a Democrat to "be a Republican" does not make much sense. And the public rejected such a plea. Only at the very end of the campaign, when Governor Dukakis began to articulate a different, more progressive agenda, did he begin to rise in the polls. But by then it was too little, too late.

Moving to the center, I will argue, is precisely the wrong thing for the Democrats to do. In fact, the best political strategy for the Democrats is to embrace their own liberal, progressive tradition and move to the left. And such an embrace must be a long-term commitment, not a strategy to win a single election. Those who argue the Democrats should move to the center and moderate their appeal and that the realities of the 1990s make a liberal agenda impossible are mistaken. Such views are based on the acceptance of a number of myths about the state of American public opinion and the Democratic "New Deal coalition":

- The public supports the Reagan-Bush agenda.
- The public has become more conservative.
- The public does not like liberals.
- The public will not tolerate any new taxes.
- The electoral college makes a liberal Democratic victory impossible.
- The New Deal coalition is dead.

None of these propositions, I will argue, is true. Some may be partially true, but basing political strategy on half-truths and myths is not likely to lead to victory. Instead, it will lead to continued defeat. Better political strategy will come from a better understanding of what the public mood actually is and what the real roadblocks are to progressive Democratic success.

Furthermore, better political strategy requires a longer view of the situation than just what might "win the next election." Rebuilding a progressive coalition will take time. Part of the problem for the Democrats, I will argue, is that the public image of the party is one of weakness and vacillation. The Democrats need, therefore, to push for a progressive, liberal agenda consistently. Even if they use such a strategy in 1992 and fail, they should not abandon it. In fact, they should consider such a loss the groundwork for a victory in 1996, just as Ronald Reagan's loss of the Republican nomination in 1976 to Gerald Ford laid the groundwork for his victory four years later. One of Ronald Reagan's and the Republican's strengths politically was the public's sense of where they stood on the issues. And that image allowed Reagan to claim a policy mandate for his victory in 1980 and push for fundamental changes in domestic and military spending and in cutting taxes. As I hope to show, given public support for a broad range of progressive policies, a strong commitment to a progressive vision over time can only enhance the Democratic Party's long-term prospects.

Similarly, simply winning a single election is not enough. If the Democrats "move to the center" and win (because, for example, there is so much unhappiness with the way things are going under President Bush), they will not have built the public support needed to make major changes in the current Republican agenda. If they win by saying "we do not want to make major changes, we will simply be more competent than the Republicans have been," then the public will not be open to major changes in health care, the environment, or other areas where progressive Democrats have a popular agenda, because the sources of opposition to such changes will still remain strongly in place. Those sources, as I hope to make clear, are strong and cannot be ignored, and the most important of them is the distrust of and alienation from government that is felt by so many people today. Progressive government requires that people trust government to solve the problems that they want solved. And, therefore, rebuilding trust in government is essential for the long-term prospects of progressive politics.

Thus, a long-term progressive strategy, I will argue, is the best way to break these barriers and change the direction of American politics. They will not simply disappear if we happen to elect a Democratic President. Even if we elect a liberal Democratic President, breaking down these barriers must be an essential part of the new administration's goals. If we do not revitalize the connections which people feel with their government, I will argue, any Democratic victory (liberal or moderate) is likely to be a hollow one. Building a progressive coalition which can continue to govern and move the country in a progressive direction requires a long-term strategy. That strategy requires clearly promoting such an agenda during the campaign and then, when victorious, beginning to implement the kinds of policies which can reconnect people with the political world.

What the Democrats need, then, is a clear, consistent, long-term progressive strategy. They need, first, to clarify what they stand for and why. If they do, they will find a great deal of public support. The public may be unhappy with the leadership choices the Democrats have offered in recent elections, and they may not like "liberals" as much as they like "conservatives," but they are supportive of a wide-range of progressive policy options. And second, the Democrats need to implement the kinds of policies which can help overcome the barriers that stand in the way of a full public embrace of a progressive agenda. Only a long-term strategy which follows both of these courses—appealing to strength and overcoming weakness—can put progressive politics on solid ground.

However, before looking at the myths of American politics in the 1990s and how they often push the Democrats away from a progressive political strategy, I need to define briefly what I mean by "progressive politics." I use the terms "liberal" and "progressive" interchangeably throughout the book. And by liberal or progressive policies I mean policies which rely on active government (as opposed to the private sector) to solve social problems and policies which are designed to represent the interests of lower-, working-, and middle-class Americans. Progressive or liberal policies are policies which place a high priority on achieving a more egalitarian society. Progressive or liberal policies use government as an instrument by which the public can express and carry out its collective wishes. Government, then, should be active and involved. Furthermore, progressives and liberals want to empower the public to allow it to make effective use of government.

I will not, in these pages, argue the philosophical truth of the liberal or progressive tradition. Rather, what I am concerned with here is showing that progressive policies make good politics.

There is a vast residue of support from the public for the kind of government envisioned by the progressive liberal tradition.

This is not to say there are not obstacles to achieving these goals as well. There are some attitudes the public holds (such as distrust of the federal government) which clearly stand in the way of building a more permanent progressive majority. But effective policies and effective politics can help to overcome these obstacles. Democrats should not be afraid to show their true colors.

Our first task must be to understand the American public. That is what we shall try to do in Part One of the book. In Chapter 2 we will look at how people relate to the world of politics and explore the myth that television is the source of political appeal. Ronald Reagan, I will argue, was not popular because he was a good television personality, but because of the perceived success of his economic policies. Furthermore, the public was always able to separate its views of Ronald Reagan the person from its political judgments of him. "Style" *does* matter to the public. They *do* judge political leaders by the way they act. But this does not mean that media presence is all that matters. Rather, I will argue, a complete understanding of the way the public relates to politics makes clear that it is *actual political performance* which the public is attempting to measure, and a reliance on style without substance is, therefore, doomed to failure.

In Chapters 3 and 4 we will explore how liberal or conservative the public actually is. We will look at what people mean when they say someone is a liberal or a conservative and how that relates to their own positions on the issues. The public does not like liberals as much as it likes conservatives, but it still likes liberal policies more than it likes conservative policies. Similarly, while it is true that the public is unhappy with the tax system, a closer look at public attitudes on taxes will show that the public is more open on this issue than we usually suppose. People do recognize the need to pay for programs they support, and they are not uniformly opposed to any rise in taxes. We need to get past the myth of a more conservative public to understand the potential for liberal, progressive policies.

In Part Two, we will turn to the Democratic coalition. Chapter 5 explores the electoral college and the argument that a progressive, liberal Democrat could never put together a geographical coalition with an electoral college majority. Evidence from statewide voting for senatorial and gubernatorial races, however, clearly shows this is not the case. A liberal Democrat can build an electoral college majority. In fact, I will argue, trying to moderate Democratic appeals to win electoral votes in the South and/or West is precisely the wrong strategy.

Chapters 6 and 7 turn to the current party coalitions. We will explore the myth that the New Deal coalition is dead and that a new Republican majority has begun to emerge. We will find, instead, that with some important changes in the South, the outline of the Democratic New Deal coalition is still in place and that strong progressive politics can help pull that coalition back together. We will, further, look at a variety of sources of cohesion and conflict both in the Democratic Party and in the Republican Party. Understanding Republican weaknesses is as important to Democratic success as is understanding Democratic strengths.

In Part Three we will turn to the kind of agenda which can rebuild a progressive Democratic coalition. In Chapter 8 we look at the kinds of policies which the Democrats can articulate to bring people back to the Democratic Party. I will argue that the Democrats need policies which address the actual concerns of people in their day-to-day lives, and, thus, part of what is needed is a politics which links national level policy to local concerns. Making politics matter to people is the only way to rebuild the links between the public and the government, and such links are necessary to sustain progressive politics in the long run. Furthermore, I will argue that clear articulation of progressive policies can help to overcome the image problems that seem to plague liberal Democrats.

Finally, in Chapter 9, we will look at the ways in which the Democratic Party can rebuild itself into the kind of widespread, grass-roots organization which can draw people back to its ranks. We will also look at the relation between the issue of party building and the need for money and how the Democrats can avoid the potential conflicts that such a need may create.

A revitalized Democratic Party can empower the public and lead to a revitalized democracy where people feel connected with, and a part of, their government. That is the type of society to which I aspire, and my hope is that the Democratic Party can move in the direction necessary to bring about such a result. What I desire to show here is that such a move can, in fact, lead to political success for the Democrats. Ten years of Ronald Reagan and George Bush has not left the public more conservative. It has left a public alienated from its government and disconnected from its political system. This is both the Democrats' biggest roadblock to success and the source of their potential strength. They need to tap into that dissatisfaction and reroute it into support for a different kind of politics from what we have seen in the United States for a long time, a politics based on the inclusion of all people in society in the collective decisions which affect their lives. In the pages that come, I hope to outline how, specifically, the Democrats can reconnect politics to people's lives by practicing such a politics of inclusion. But first we need to turn to a look at how, exactly, people do relate to the political world.

A Postscript on Perot

Toward the end of the 1992 presidential primary season, as this book goes to press in June, the unexpected public support for the independent presidential campaign of Texas billionaire H. Ross Perot has startled the political world. His campaign obviously has relevance for the argument made in these pages. The most striking thing about the Perot campaign is the way that it taps into the feelings of alienation and distrust that I posit provide both the opportunity for, and the major obstacle to, progressive Democrats. People are fed up with "the system." They think that it is not working, and they want a change. On the other hand, they still believe that a properly functioning government can solve many of the problems America faces. They think that the right leader can straighten things out and get the country moving again. This desire to be part of an effective governmental system is, in many ways, fueling the Perot campaign. People see him as something different, someone who can return government to the people.

Obviously, I lack the space to go into detail here. But it is clear to me that while H. Ross Perot, by tapping into some of the trends I outline, may be able to win support for his presidential campaign, his effort is a singular, nationally focused phenomenon which lacks the local organization and roots to build the kind of long-term progressive coalition I describe in this book. I argue that the Democratic Party needs to reconnect people with their government and make them feel a part of the system. Only then can a strong, long-term progressive governing coalition rule. Winning the presidency alone is not enough. Building strong, progressive Democratic Party organizations at the local level is not enough. Only by doing both can we stimulate the kind of support for government which is necessary if a popular progressive agenda is to be implemented.

The phenomenon of H. Ross Perot, if anything, makes this even more imperative, for his success would only be one side of the equation, the presidential side. Such success by itself, in my view, would make the other side—building local organizations with which people feel connected—more difficult, something I fear would set back the long-term prospects of building a truly progressive governing coalition. In the pages that follow, I hope to show what the real sources of strength and of weakness are for progressive politics in this country, and how, in the 1992 election and beyond, the Democratic Party can rebuild itself accordingly.

I should also note that Perot's candidacy has obvious implications for the electoral college strategy I outline in Chapter 5. What he does in that regard is to open things up. If he runs, no state is safe for either the Democrats or the Republicans. Thus, a progressive Democrat clearly could win an electoral college majority with Perot on the ballot. And my longer term point—that there are enough states with a history of supporting progressive Democrats to make a "move to the center" unnecessary if the Democrats want to capture the White House—is still a valid one.

Part One

The American Public in the 1990s: Myths and Realities

2

What Matters to People: The Myth of Charisma in American Politics

We often hear the argument that contemporary American politics is dominated by style or form, not content. The images we see on television dominate our view of politics. Pictures and symbols are more important than the content of policy. Candidates present thirty-second commercials. The evening news gives us two-minute (or ten-second!) stories. In such an environment, it becomes difficult to deal adequately with real problems and concerns.

The "Teflon Presidency" of Ronald Reagan was the clearest metaphor for this position. No matter what substantive problems arose, a clever sound-bite, a good picture, and the personal popularity of Ronald Reagan were able to wipe it away. Personality, "charisma," is what it takes to lead the country. If you have that, all is forgiven. Similarly, many analysts have argued that George Bush defeated Michael Dukakis because he was able to create a more positive image of himself. Kirk O'Donnell, a senior Dukakis adviser, for example, said, "The long and the short of it is, the Bush campaign ran a better campaign than we did." And one of Dukakis' key aides, John Sasso, said, "[The Democrats] have to be able to compete with what is a very effective team of people on the other side that understands communications, that understands the symbols of the country."[1] If Dukakis had not come across as so stiff and unemotional, if he could have made better use of the symbols of the nation, he might have won the election.

It is my contention that this view of American politics is incorrect. Style or form does matter. It has to, in an environment dominated by television. But in the end, content is the key. Ronald Reagan was popular as a President because people thought his policies were working fairly well. If that had not been true, the personal appeal he had could not have been transferred into a political appeal. Dukakis did come across as stiff and unemotional. But there were more substantial, political reasons why he lost the election. Bush did run a better campaign, and Dukakis could have made better use of the symbols of American politics, but focusing on such matters will not cure the ills of the Democratic Party.

If the Democratic Party is to rebuild itself, it needs to understand the true sources of Ronald Reagan's appeal and the true reasons why Michael Dukakis lost the 1988 election. If the Democrats accept the myth of the primacy of style, they are doomed to failure. Trying to be better at creating images which suit Republican interests is, in the long run, impossible. Even if the Democrats were to win an election or two under those conditions, they would be in no position to promote the kinds of policies which can allow them to build a more permanent governing coalition.

There is some truth to the argument that style is important. But as we will see, it is only half true. And accepting the half for the whole is a dangerous game for the Democrats. In this chapter then, we will explore the importance of image and symbol in contemporary American politics and look at how people actually do try to relate to the world of politics.

The Sources of Presidential Appeal

Ronald Reagan was not a particularly popular President. His approval ratings, as measured by the Gallup Poll, were certainly not

Table 2-1

Ronald Reagan's Approval Ratings, 1981–1988 (in percent)

Date of Survey	Approve	Date of Survey	Approve
1981 March	60	1985 March	56
June	59	June	58
September	52	September	60
December	49	December	63
1982 March	46	1986 March	63
June	44	June	64
September	42	September	61
December	41	December	47
1983 March	41	1987 March	46
June	42	June	53
September	48	August	49
December	54	December	49
1984 March	54	1988 March	51
June	54	June	51
September	57	September	54
December	59	December	63

Percentages are the responses to the question: "Do you approve or disapprove of the way Ronald Reagan is handling his job as President?" Data for this table come from *The Gallup Report*, July 1988, p. 20 and October 1988, p. 26, and *American Public Opinion Data, 1989*, Opinion Research Service, microfiche card #40.

higher, and in many cases were actually lower, than those of his predecessors. What, in fact, was different in President Reagan's popularity ratings is the pattern of support they show. Most Presidents' approval ratings have followed a pattern of decreasing support through the course of their Presidency. In Reagan's case, however, the pattern of support began with an initial decline but then reversed itself, rose substantially, went through a second period of decline, and finally rose again.[2] (See Table 2-1). What struck many observers about the rise in support that began in 1983 was that the public was willing to express approval for President Reagan in spite of opposing many of his specific policies. This led to the view that the President's popularity was a function of his image, not his policies. For example, writing in the *New York Times*, Steven Weisman wrote that Ronald Reagan had:

> . . . committed untold public bloopers and been caught in dozens of factual mistakes and misrepresentations. He has presided over the worst recession since the Great Depression. The abortive mission in Beirut cost 265 American lives, and there has been a sharp escalation in United States military involvement in Central America. An extraordinary number of Mr. Reagan's political appointees have come under fire, with many forced to resign, because of ethical or legal conflicts. Yet he is the man in the Teflon Suit; nothing sticks to him.[3]

But it was not Ronald Reagan's image that led to the revival in his popularity, it was the perception that the economy was getting better. Support for Ronald Reagan in his first term mirrored changes in the unemployment rate. When unemployment went up, the President's popularity went down. When unemployment declined, Reagan's popularity grew. In a careful study of the sources of presidential popularity, Charles Ostrom and Dennis Simon conclude:

> the economy and public concerns about economic problems are the dominant influences on public support for President Reagan. The estimates also reveal that the impact of presidentially relevant events is considerable. This implies that sequential events (e.g. the Iran-Contra affair) or a series of unrelated but closely spaced events (e.g., KAL 007, Lebanon, and Grenada in the fall of 1983) have the capacity to alter the shape or path of public support. However, the same cannot be said for speeches and trips, the more controllable forms of drama.[4]

And other scholars studying this issue have come to similar conclusions.[5] Events in the political environment are what drive people to express support for the President. In this regard, it is also interesting to note that the public has always been able to separate its view of Reagan the man from its view of Reagan the

Table 2-2

Ronald Reagan's Personal Popularity, 1981–1988 (in percent)

Date of Survey	Approve	Disapprove	No opinion
1988 December	79	13	8
1987 July	72	21	6
April	75	18	7
February	71	23	6
January	74	18	8
1986 December	75	18	7
September	80	12	8
1985 November	81	10	9
1983 August	67	21	12
1982 November	73	17	10
February	70	20	10
1981 July	78	13	9
April	69	19	12

Percentages are the responses to the question: "Apart from whether you approve or disapprove of the way Reagan is handling his job as President, what do you think of Ronald Reagan as a person?" Data for this table come from *The Gallup Report*, July 1987, p. 4, and *American Public Opinion Data, 1989,* Opinion Research Service, microfiche card #40.

President. As can be seen in Table 2-2, the public has always liked Ronald Reagan the person, even at times when it has not liked the job he was doing in office. This personal popularity is important. It is something that a President can draw upon. When things go well, it will make it easier for the public to be supportive. When things go badly, it may temper public displeasure and give a President some breathing room. But the point is that in the end, realities of the political world win out. Content is the key. Without the substance, the form is irrelevant.

The dominance of content over style can also be seen in public attitudes toward Oliver North and U.S. policy in Nicaragua. North testified before Congress in July 1987 about his role in the

Table 2-3

Public Support for the Nicaraguan Contras (in percent)

Date of Survey	Favor Aid	Oppose aid	Don't know
April 1986	28	65	7
June 1986	29	62	9
January 1987	23	70	7
January 1987*	28	62	10
March 1987	28	67	5
May 1987	28	67	5
July 1987	42	46	12
August 1987	37	59	6
January 1988*	30	57	13

Data from the ABC/*Washington Post* poll, cited in *Public Opinion*, September/October 1987, p. 24, and, for the two dates marked with an *, from an NBC News poll cited in *American Public Opinion Data*, 1988, Opinion Research Service, microfiche card #72. For the ABC/*Washington Post* poll, percentages are responses to the question, "Do you generally favor or oppose the U.S. [Congress] granting [$100 million] in military (and other) aid to the Nicaraguan rebels known as the Contras?" For the NBC News poll, the question was, "Do you favor or oppose the U.S. government giving money for military aid to the rebels fighting the government in Nicaragua?"

Iran-Contra scandals. In spite of vast publicity, favorable coverage, and some media reports that Oliver North was a new "national hero," a July 9, 1987 CBS/*New York Times* poll found that only 18 percent of the American public felt North was a hero. And this number was almost identical to the number (14 percent) that felt he was a hero in a Gallup survey done shortly after North's 1989 conviction (later overturned) on charges arising from the Iran-Contra fiasco.[6]

It is not that the people did not like Oliver North. They did. Most, according to Gallup, felt he was misguided in his judgment. And the public did respond to North's engaging testimony. Tom Brokaw declared that North had hit a "grand slam" and went on to praise the colonel's "performance" after the first morning of his testimony. But television's obsession with form over content is not the public's obsession. The public watched the testimony, liked North, and concluded that what he had done was not heroic.

In fact, public opinion on U.S. involvement in Nicaragua and public perceptions of the Contras, the anti-Sandinista rebels, were not altered by North's testimony. As Table 2-3 shows, while there was an increase in public support for the Contras immediately following North's television appearance, the increase was small (and those supporting aiding the Contras never outnumbered those opposing aid), and temporary. Public opposition to funding the Contras quickly returned to pre–North testimony levels. Again, the point is that people's views of politics are not easily swayed by "form." It is the content of policy that, in the end, leads to their judgments.

This myth of the primacy of form is largely a function of two half-truths. The first of these half-truths is that citizens do not experience the world of politics directly. In contemporary America, the institutional realities of the world of politics come to people through television and newspapers. The realities of such politics are *mediated* realities.[7] Thus, the argument goes, political images on the television screen become the realities of politics. Flag-waving, patriotic speeches, and the variety of symbols suggesting national strength obscure the American reality of increasing poverty, inequality, and racism. This particular social reality is hidden from many Americans by the political images they consume. A master of communication like Ronald Reagan used his ability to manipulate images and make people feel good about the nation, masking our real social problems.[8]

The second half-truth involves the way the media cover the world of politics. As has been shown by a number of observers, the media, and television in particular, respond to organizational imperatives when making decisions about how to show the "news."[9] Such imperatives lead to a presentation of the news that is based on a series of disconnected stories, each partially sensationalized in an attempt to entertain people and give them a story which is a self-contained whole.

There is, then, no ideology (at least explicitly) to tie together the news that people watch. The news itself becomes another commodity that is sold. People are left without any framework for judging what they have seen. And this, in turn, leaves people vulnerable to a politics of style. If the media focus on the question of whether George Bush "came across well" in his debate with Michael Dukakis, that is what the public will focus on as well. What is missing from these half-truths (and from views of presidential popularity as based on image), however, is an adequate understanding of how people try to make sense of the world of politics.

How People Make Sense of the World of Politics

It is true that most people do get their information about politics from the mass media and, therefore, are likely to be influenced by the images and stories they see on the screen. People do not, however, rely solely or primarily on such information to make political judgments. Rather, political consciousness is formed primarily by personal political experience. How people think is shaped primarily by how they live. The power of the media is real only insofar as it appears to confirm our own reality. Numerous studies have shown that the media do not change people's minds about issues.[10]

Experience serves as a "reality check" in judging the networks political reports. The most important reality check appears to be the state of the economy. If more people are being laid off or fired, those people know. If more people are losing their homes or farms, those people know. If prices are rising at the supermarket, people who shop know. Even in an area such as foreign policy that is particularly difficult to judge firsthand, the public's willingness to believe everything that the government tells them is limited, as the unpopularity of aid to the Contras indicates.

People do not watch the news "tabula rasa." While the media presentation of politics channels people to think about problems and issues in particular ways, the media do not create the context that people utilize in processing the news. The media are only the messengers. People process the message through the filter of their own political values and social experiences. And in many ways, the media recognize this. The emphasis on "human interest" stories and the personalization of the news (for example, using the story of particular individuals to tell the story of some broad social problem such as drugs, crime, or AIDS) reflect the media's understanding that people like to be able to relate to the news in a personal way. Similarly, the popularity of so-called "infotainment" shows, such as *Oprah Winfrey* or *Donahue*, reflects the desire of people to engage "significant" social issues in a personal way. Information that people can relate to through their own lives or the lives of other individuals is of greater value to people as they try to make sense of the world of politics than more general statistical information (such as the increase in the poverty rate).

Thus, people use their own lives and experiences to help them understand the world of politics. The problem with such a process, however, is that most people have only limited experiences. They may, therefore, have a difficult time understanding the realities of people who have different life experiences from their own. In a study I recently completed that relied on a series of in-depth interviews with a small group of citizens, one of the most striking things I found was the way people used their own, often limited, experiences to help them understand the world of politics.[11] So, for example, in discussing problems with welfare and food stamps, one individual I talked with (whom I call John), said:

> I used to work at the X supermarket. You know, the first of the month, man the garbage those people [food stamp recipients] would buy. And I never used to see them, in their carts, with any kind of soap in them. They used to come in with Pillsbury this. You know, there's got to be better control over what the money is being spent for.

Similarly, in describing the problem of unemployment, a women I call Sue said:

> Even people that, our friends and whatever, that have gone to college and whatever, and something happens to their job. It may not be their fault or whatever. And they accepted, well if I am on unemployment I get so much a week. If I go out and, for example, a

> school teacher, if I go out and sub every day, make $50 or $60 every day for so many days, I could make the same amount of money sitting home, so why should I go out and try and substitute. Well how are you ever gonna get another job if you want to get back into teaching. Subbing at least you are exposed and if you are good then someone will say hey, we want you the next opening. But instead they chose to be on unemployment.

Unemployment, to Sue, was a problem of professional people refusing to lower themselves, not people with no skills or training being unable to find jobs. Similarly, John's view of food stamp recipients was based on his observations of what they bought in the store. And such images are often reinforced by a media that most often portrays the reality of white middle-class men. Alternative realities are not often seen in the world of television.

People's experiences, then, shape the way they look at political issues and realities. And since most people have only limited political experiences, it is true that they are often easily swayed by anecdotal evidence that supports their own conceptions. Ronald Reagan's story of the man who bought vodka with food stamps (a story which has never been documented) or stories of Pentagon waste and corruption (such as buying expensive hammers or toilet seats) carry disproportionate weight because people often have heard or seen waste in government and government programs. I will explore, in Chapter 8, the kinds of policies and appeals the Democrats might support that can convince people of the need for programs which deal with realities many Americans never see. But, for now, the important point is that people do, in fact, rely on their own experiences whenever possible to judge the political world. And while those experiences may be limited, they do allow people to attempt to get beyond the images they see to an understanding of the content of policy.

But the use of personal experience to make sense of politics runs deeper than the attempt to judge policy. As we know, people *do* pay attention to image. Content may, in the end, win out, but people are swayed by style. Candidates for office spend an inordinate amount of time and energy trying to create "the right image." The Bush campaign was a success, we are told, in part, because the Vice-President was able to overcome his earlier image as a "wimp" (whatever that means!), while the Dukakis campaign failed to convince people that the Governor was an empathetic individual. Clearly candidates and the media focus on image. And the public does as well. When asked why they like or dislike candidates running for office, people often respond in terms of the candidate's image or style: George Bush is not tough enough; or Michael Dukakis is too wishy-washy.

Part of the reason for this reliance on style is that people often feel confused or unsure about the issues. Which candidate actually has a better plan to balance the budget? Both sides have their experts who say they are right. And if economists cannot agree, how can we expect the average citizen to know? What people *can* try to do, however, is pick the candidate they think is most likely to proceed in the proper direction. If we pick the "right kind" of leader, we will get the "right kind" of policy. Thus, many people attempt to make sense of politics and understand why some things work and some things fail, not by looking at the details of policy, but by looking at the kind of people who are in charge. If we choose experienced, strong, compassionate leaders, good results will follow. And every candidate tries to portray himself or herself in these terms.[12]

People disagree about the types of leaders they want. In fact, some of what they want may be contradictory. Some may emphasize strength; others may prefer compassion or honesty or diligence. But in making such decisions, people draw on their own experiences. We may not know what the best way is to deal with the problem of drugs or how to keep America's place in the world safe and secure, but we all know people who are successful and people who are not. And thus, as we make sense of the world of politics, we find style to be a useful guide to decisions about politics. In my in-depth interviews with people, they often would relate good leadership traits to experiences from their own life. A man I call Ed, for example, in discussing the need for a tough president, said:

I know how many times I got punched in the mouth when I was in high school, and how many times people smaller than me got punched in the mouth. And it's kind of strange. We could be sitting right next to each other. But someone would pick on them and not me. And I wasn't necessarily a part of the bully's crowd either.

Similarly, Tony told me that what he looked for in a leader was someone who is

. . . a good listener before he can be a good talker. I learned that the hard way. When I first started working, I went in with the attitude, well I knew it all. And I found out quickly, I didn't know any of it. So I reversed my whole attitude and I listened. And I listened and I listened and I listened before I spoke. So, and it helped me in the long run. And that's what I try and instill in my kids. And my wife tries to instill in me, still. But I think a good politician will listen.

And Sue told me:

Like President Reagan says, the buck stops here. And that's right. Whenever you are leading something and you are in charge, you know you get your advice from all the people around you, and the people who are around you are ones you pick and hopefully you pick the person for the job not because you owe them it. But you are the one that has to make the final decision and you are the one that is responsible. That's what I believe, you know for all the organizations that I am in, when I am in charge and I have responsibility, I feel that I am responsible for it, so therefore the buck stops here. It's important to be strong and listen to everybody's opinion, but you have to come out and make the decision. You are responsible for it.

In many ways it is easier to base stylistic judgments on one's own life experiences than it is to base policy judgments on such experiences. But the important point to remember is that these stylistic judgments are, in fact, an attempt to predict who will be a good leader. They are an attempt to produce leaders who will produce the "content" that people want. It is not simply an "image" vote.

Paradoxically, however, while it is very easy for people to base their view of what kinds of styles are important to them on their own experiences, it is very difficult for them to know if the people they have chosen use the "proper styles." We may know we want a leader to be tough. But how do we know if George Bush is tough? *Retrospective evaluations* are the best evidence people have that allows them to use their own experiences. If things are going well, the President must be tough enough. If they are not, evidently he is not tough enough and we need to find somebody tougher. My own very limited sample (as well as both the 1984 and 1988 American National Election studies) found that people who rely primarily on style in making political judgments are also much more likely to cite retrospective evaluations of the way things are going as an evaluative tool than are people who are inclined to make political judgments on the basis of the details of policy a candidate or official espouses.[13]

The importance of retrospective evaluations in people's political decisions is well-documented.[14] But what is often overlooked is the way in which these evaluations are used to confirm or deny the presence of a "proper style of politics" on the part of those who are in office. As James Ceaser notes, in looking at the ups and downs in Ronald Reagan's popularity and the different ways his style was judged over the course of his administration:

> The fact that character judgments are bound up so closely with the outcomes of events lends some support to Machiavelli's extreme formulation that, if successful, "the means will always be judged honorable and praised by everyone, for the people are always taken . . . by the outcome.[15]

We tend to assume that retrospective evaluations are "policy oriented." If things are going well, people conclude that proper policies are being pursued. And that is correct. But it misses the step in many people's reasoning which says that the proper policies are being pursued because we have the right kind of leaders. And in 1988, George Bush was able to profit from people's perceptions that things had gone relatively well under Ronald Reagan. It is true that Bush was not Reagan (and that, in fact, was something that the Democrats tried to exploit), but Bush could, and did, make the appeal that he was part of the Reagan-Bush Administration and that he would be the same kind of President that Ronald Reagan was. And as Table 2-4 shows,[16]

Table 2-4

1988 Presidential Vote by Approval of the Reagan Administration (in percent)

	Vote for Bush	Vote for Dukakis	Percentage of Total Vote
Strongly approve	90.1	9.9	36.6
Weakly approve	62.2	37.8	25.4
Weakly disapprove	21.9	78.1	13.0
Strongly disapprove	6.2	93.8	25.0

Data from the 1988 American National Election Study.

approval of Ronald Reagan was a strong factor in distinguishing Bush voters from Dukakis voters.

The importance of all this, then, is twofold. First, the public does, in fact, try to make sense of politics by looking at content, not style. But since public information is limited, style is often used as a way to judge future content. People reason that if we choose leaders with the right kinds of styles or images, we will get good policies. Image, therefore, is important but only because of its perceived relation to content. And as opinion on Nicaragua and the Contras shows, people's underlying attitudes toward particular policies are also an important constraint on what leaders can do. Even if you have "the right image," the public will not accept everything you want to do. The public has never, for example, been happy with George Bush's domestic agenda in spite of its approval of his foreign policy initiatives and his overall popularity. Thus, for example, an October 1991 *Washington Post*/ABC News Poll found that while 69 percent of the public approved of President Bush's handling of international relations and 65 percent approved of his performance overall, only 37 percent approved of his handling of the economy.[17] In the end, people look for results. The popularity of leaders is dependent on their ability to produce. Image can only take them a limited way.

And second, the information people trust most is information that comes out of their own experiences. People look to what happens in their lives, the people they come in contact with, and the policy outcomes they can see in tangible (even if unrepresentative) ways. If the Democrats do not recognize this, they are doomed to failure. They cannot simply run "image campaigns" and hope to win. If they try to be "better Republicans" (that is, if they try to say that "the real issue is competence" not differences in policy, as Michael Dukakis did in 1988), they are bound to fail, because people will see no reason to change. And if things turn bad and they do win a presidential election because they are perceived as being "more competent," the public will not be prepared to accept major changes in policy. If they want to rebuild a long-term governing coalition, the Democrats need to create a clear, strong alternative image that contrasts with the Republicans.

What the Democrats need to do is create this proper image by arguing for policies which will make a difference in people's lives, policies which will affect the experiences people have and allow them to build long-term support for the party. They need to make politics matter to people. But before we move to a look at people's attitudes on policy issues (the raw material Democrats have to build upon), there is one more element we need to add to this equation: people's general attitude toward government, and the lack of trust they exhibit in that respect.

Attitudes Toward Government: The Lack of Public Trust

One of the major problems facing the Democratic Party is the public's lack of trust in the government and the view (correct, I might add) that the Democrats are the party of "big government." As Table 2-5 shows, the decline in levels of trust in the government to do what is right most or all of the time did reverse itself in the Reagan years, but even now a majority of the public distrusts the government In 1988, 64 percent of the public thought the federal government was too powerful, and only 13 percent of the public thought that the government pays attention to what people think "a good deal of the time." As Jean Bethke Elshtain

Table 2-5

Trust in Government, 1958–1988 (in percent)

Year	Level of Trust	Year	Level of Trust
1958	73	1976	33
1964	76	1976	30
1966	65	1980	26
1968	61	1982	34
1970	54	1984	45
1972	53	1986	39
1974	37	1988	41

Percentage is those trusting the government in Washington to do the right thing all or most of the time. Data come from the American National Election Series. (The question was not asked in 1960 or 1962.)

noted in describing the state of public opinion in 1988:

> Public opinion polls have indicated for a number of years that a solid majority of Americans favor national health insurance of some sort, job guarantees, and more protection of the environment. But equally solid majorities believe the federal government is too large, spends too much, and intrudes too directly into people's lives.[18]

The problem, then, for the Democrats, is to overcome this residue of mistrust of government to build support for particular policies to deal with the problems facing the nation. (We will look at public attitudes in specific policy areas in the next two chapters.) Public support for action in general on social issues is too often counterbalanced by opposition to actual government activity. The public wants the government to do things to solve the problems they see. But when a specific program is proposed, it is easy to build opposition to it as "another example of throwing money at problems" or "another government program filled with waste and corruption."

Ironically, the Reagan years have helped the Democrats in this regard. Public trust in government is higher than it has been in two decades. Ronald Reagan has shown the public that government can work. But the Democrats need to be careful to support the kinds of policies which will build public support for government, not resentment at the activities of a far-off government.

The public finds it very difficult to relate to the government in Washington. In 1988, 70 percent of the public agreed with the statement that "sometimes politics and government seem so complicated that a person like me can't really understand what's going on." So when people can find something that makes sense to them, such as the fact that there is waste and corruption, that often plays a central role in their thinking about politics.[19] For a party which supports active government, such attitudes among the public are problematic. Part of the Democratic agenda, therefore, must be to connect people back with their government. The Democrats need to build trust and support not only in the particular leaders and policies they offer to the public, but also in the process of popular government. Such a change will not be easy to accomplish. But nobody said building a strong long-term coalition in favor of active governmental policies to promote social justice and change would be easy. The types of policies and proposals which might help accomplish this will be discussed in the final part of this book. For now we simply need to note the difficulty that the distance from, and distrust of, government places in the way of a progressive agenda.

Conclusion

The experiences that people have in their lives are central to the way they think about the world. Since most people do not "experience" politics directly, they attempt to make indirect connections between the events and people they meet in their lives and what happens in the political world. Judgments of "style" are one such attempt. Retrospective evaluations about the way things, particularly the economy, are going, are another.

Television does, then, play an important role in people's evaluations of politics and political figures. And the stylistic impressions that people form of candidates do make a difference. But style by itself is not enough. In the end, the public demands results. The public always thought Ronald Reagan was a nice person. But they only approved of his Presidency when they thought things were going well. The same can be said of George Bush. As the public turned its attention away from the "success of Operation Desert Storm" and toward the "failures" present in the United States, Bush's approval ratings declined. The right "form" can get one started, but only the right "content" can lead to longer-term public support.

The Democrats do need, therefore, to be "stylistically correct." But as I hope to show, they can be stylistically correct while still pursuing a political agenda which involves redistributing wealth; helping the underprivileged; increasing opportunities for women, African-Americans, and other minority groups; cleaning up the environment; improving social services; and championing social justice. "Style" or "charisma" is not policy specific. More importantly, it is in the end less important than the results of the policies that are in fact implemented. And there is a great deal of public support for the kinds of policies the Democrats espouse (or should espouse). If the Democrats push for their agenda in a clear, consistent way, if they show strength in their convictions and compassion in their policies, then they can build support for the kinds of changes they recommend.

It is also important to remember that just as "having the right image" is not enough, "being popular" is also not enough to convince the public that one's policy recommendations are correct. The public was unmoved by eight years of Reagan Administration support for the Contra rebels in Nicaragua. The result was the inability of the Reagan Administration to convince Congress to go along with it on this issue. The public approved of Ronald Reagan because it approved of the way the economy was progressing. And because of that, it tolerated its differences with him on, as we shall see, a wide range of policies. As Chapter 3 will document, what this means for the Democrats is that in a large number of areas, the public is already on their side. If Democrats can convince the public of their capacity to govern, and, of course, once they are back in power, if the public perceives Democratic policies as successful, there is the potential to build a long-term, strong, progressive coalition in the United States.

For that to happen, however, the Democrats need to rebuild people's connections with government. They need policies which promote the values and ideals of the party and do not seem to impose government from Washington "on the backs of the people." Rebuilding such connections will, in the end, be the strongest weapon for the Democrats in building a strong governing coalition, for such connections will allow people to experience government more directly and, therefore, to rely even less on the images they see on their television screen and more on themselves. But before we turn to the kinds of policies which might create such connections, we need to explore the current state of public opinion on a range of domestic and foreign policy issues. There is already a great deal of support for a "liberal" political agenda, and even on the issues of taxes, things are not as bleak as conventional wisdom would have us believe.

3

The "L" Word:
The Myth of the Death
of Liberalism

The 1988 presidential campaign was marked by unprecedented attacks on "liberals" as being out of touch with mainstream America. And, in fact, only 23 percent of the American public classified themselves as liberals in the 1988 American National Election Study, the smallest number to do so since the question was introduced in the early 1970s.[1] Liberals felt under siege and on the defensive. But George Bush's attacks on "liberal ideas" were misplaced. It is true that the public does not like "liberals" as much as it likes "conservatives." But that was true even in the "liberal" 1960s. What is not true is that the public does not like "liberal" policies.

The Meaning of "Liberal"

For most people, the term "liberal" is not a set of policy positions. In fact, the lack of correlation between people's self-placement on the liberal-conservative scale and their issue positions has attracted the attention of political analysts for quite some time.[2] When people say they are liberals or conservatives, very few of them mean to say that they support a series of policy positions which political pundits and analysts label as liberal or conservative. Rather, these words have much more of a symbolic meaning. And my conversations with people indicate that for many the symbolism has to do with the same kinds of stylistic concerns I discussed in the previous chapter.[3] People like or dislike liberals because they see them as certain types of people. For example, John, a twenty-seven-year old college graduate I spoke with, said he did not like liberals because a liberal was "someone who will not really stay stable on their views. You know. Move either way. To and fro."

In contrast, Ralph, a twenty-eight-year old manual laborer with a high school education, liked liberals because they are "more open or more for the people. More listen to the people, to their views and their ideas."

It is the supposed styles of liberals and conservatives which many (though not all) people are responding to when they react to these symbols. And in this way of looking at the world, liberals are often seen as "wishy-washy" or "too willing to change things" or "not stable enough," while conservatives are seen as "consistent" or "clear" or "getting back to basics."

In addition, those who do identify these symbolic words with particular policy positions and not with styles usually do not identify them with a broad range of policy positions but rather with a more narrow set of policies. A liberal may be someone who is in favor of abortion rights or civil rights. Or a liberal may be someone who favors government spending. Or a liberal may be someone who supports a less aggressive foreign policy. But only a small percentage of the public sees a liberal as someone who believes all of these things.[4] And therefore, when people do not like "liberals" they are rarely condemning the broad range of policies we identify as liberal.

As Table 3-1 makes clear, the public's preference for conservatives over liberals is a long-standing one. But that does not now indicate, nor has ever indicated, a preference for conservative policies over liberal ones. Writing in 1968, Free and Cantril noted that Americans were philosophically conservative and op-

Table 3-1

Feelings About Liberals and Conservatives, 1964–1988

Year	Liberals	Conservatives
1964	53	57
1968	51	57
1972	53	60
1976	52	58
1980	51	61
1984	56	60
1988	52	61

Figures are the mean feeling thermometer scores for liberals and conservatives. Feeling thermometers run from "0" for very cold (negative) feelings, through "50" for neutral feelings, to "100" for very warm (positive) feelings. The data are from the American National Election Study series.

erationally liberal.[5] To that, I would add that Americans are "stylistically conservative" as well. But as we shall see, they are still "operationally liberal." Liberals do, therefore, have an image problem. A candidate who calls himself or herself a "conservative" is likely to have a larger natural constituency than a candidate who calls himself or herself a "liberal." But it is a problem which has more to do with a perception of style than one of policy. Celinda Lake and Stanley Greenberg, for example, found that 58 percent of the public felt "sides too much with minorities" is a good or very good description of a liberal, 42 percent felt "naive about foreign threats" is a good or very good description of a liberal, and 37 percent felt "does not support strong enough moral standards" is a good or very good description of a liberal.[6] These views of liberals represent a view of a particular type of person, not one who supports particular policies. The wrong approach to solving this problem, then, is to try to become more "conservative" on the issues. That will not help. (In fact, as we shall see, it will often make the problem worse.) The right approach is to redefine the stylistic images of liberals and conservatives. I will return to this point shortly. But before we do that, we need a closer look at the "operational liberalism" of the

American public. In a policy sense, how "liberal" or "conservative" is the American public? (I will defer discussion of taxing and spending issues until the next chapter.)

Where Americans Stand on the Issues

The Reagan era has seen Americans either maintain the progressive policy positions they have always held or move consistently *to the left* on a broad range of issues. Even as early as 1982, it was clear to those who looked at public opinion data that the public was not, in fact, becoming more conservative.[7] The public has been, and is, strongly supportive of liberal policy positions over a wide range of areas.

Economic and Social Welfare Policy

The public strongly supports government involvement in the economy and strong regulation of business activity. For example, between 1969 and 1979, the percentage of people agreeing with the statement that "there is too much power concentrated in the hands of a few large companies for the good of the nation" increased from 69 percent to 79 percent, and the percentage agreeing that government should put a limit on the profits that companies make increased from 33 percent to 50 percent.[8] Similarly, in 1985, 75 percent of the public felt it was the government's responsibility to keep prices under control.[9] And in 1988, when given a choice between the position that government should take a strong role in the economy to provide prosperity and the position that government should regulate and tax less in order to ensure a prosperous economy, 64 percent of the public (including 58 percent of self-described conservatives) chose the first option.[10]

The public, then, at least in the abstract, supports the idea of strong government activity to help keep the economy moving. Less regulation and less intervention are not the favored course of action. This can also be seen in public support for protecting

Table 3-2

Confidence in Labor and Business, 1973–1988 (in percent)

Year	Labor	Business	Year	Labor	Business
1973	30	26	1984	30	29
1975	38	34	1985	28	31
1977	39	33	1986	29	28
1979	36	32	1987	26	NA
1981	28	20	1988	26	25
1983	26	28			

Percentages are those saying they had a great deal or quite a lot of confidence in organized labor or big business. Data come from *The Gallup Report*, December 1988, p. 30.

American jobs from foreign competition through tougher trade laws (59 percent of the public felt this should be an important goal of the Bush Administration!)[11] and in public support for raising the minimum wage (in May 1988, 76 percent of the public supported raising the minimum wage to more than $5.00 over a four-year period.)[12] And while the public is quite skeptical of organized labor (a skepticism which has grown since the 1970s), it is at least as skeptical of big business. (See Table 3-2). The problem for the Democrats, then, is not a lack of public support for strong intervention in the economy, but the same lack of trust in government to do the right thing that I discussed in Chapter 2. The public likes the idea of government looking out for its welfare, but it is skeptical of the ability of government to do so efficiently and fairly. Rebuilding that trust, again, is the major task facing the Democratic Party.

A similar pattern exists in social welfare policy. People agree that it is government's responsibility to care for the needy. But they see current welfare programs as riddled with waste and corruption and are, therefore, leery of increasing government aid. Thus, for example, Lake and Greenberg found that when given a choice between the options of having government stay out of families' lives and letting people get ahead on their own, or helping families even if that means increasing government spending in areas like child care or health care, 51 percent of the public favored the latter option.[13] And the 1988 American National Election Study found that 42 percent of the public felt it was government's responsibility to provide health insurance for individuals (with 39 percent saying health insurance should be left up to private industry and 19 percent undecided). And John Doble and Keith Melville, using a quota sample of 545 people taking part in a three-hour-long session designed to probe attitudes on social welfare policy, found that "the majority view is that government should do more for the poor, especially for poor children."[14]

On the other hand, people do not like current welfare programs. Survey data consistently show that "welfare" is one of the two areas of public spending people are most willing to cut (foreign aid is the other one).[15] The welfare program is seen as riddled with fraud and corruption. One of the individuals I interviewed put it this way:

> "We have got to have rules in place about going up to the track and betting ten dollars on one horse, somebody on welfare doing that. Then they are crying that they are not getting enough. I think that's one issue that we have to get a lot more stern on. I don't mind paying for people who are less fortunate. But use it to put a clean shirt on someone's back, not to bet ten bucks on the three horse."

In fact, two-thirds of the people I talked with raised the issue of the fairness of the current welfare system.[16] And Doble and Melville also found widespread dissatisfaction with current government antipoverty programs.[17] Thus, in the area of economic and social welfare policy, the problem for the Democrats is clear. (The issue of taxes will be taken up in Chapter 4.) The public must be convinced that the kinds of solutions and policies Democrats offer will not result in more bloated, unresponsive, wasteful government. The public does not support the Republican view that most of these problems are best left to an unregulated, free economy. But they are leery of the ability of government to do much good. I hope to show, in Chapter 8, how the Democrats can rebuild the kind of trust necessary to turn this theoretical public support into a strong constituency in favor of activist government.

Environmental Policy

Public opinion on environmental policy is much less ambiguous. The public is strongly supportive of governmental action to clean up our air, water, and land. For example, Lake and Greenberg found that 73 percent of the public felt that imposing stricter environmental regulations on corporations which produce toxic waste should be a very important priority of the Bush Administration.[18] Similarly, the Gallup Poll found that 79 percent of the public supported banning ozone-depleting chemicals and that 76 percent of the public thought of themselves as environmentalists. And as Table 3-3 indicates, the public claims, at least, to worry quite a bit about environmental issues.[19] When asked if the government should relax pollution controls to reduce costs to industry, 67 percent of the public said "no" in 1988 (up slightly from the 64 percent who said "no" in 1984), while an April 1991 poll found that 71 percent of the public felt we should protect the environment even if that led to the curbing of economic growth.[20]

Support for nuclear power has also declined over the past fifteen years. In 1976, 34 percent of the public felt it was extremely important to build more nuclear power plants while only 8 percent of the public felt it was not at all important. By 1986, those figures were 14 percent feeling it was extremely important and 26 percent feeling it was not at all important. And two-thirds of the public in 1986 felt that we should hold off on building more nuclear power plants until stricter safety regulations could be worked out.[21]

Clearly, then, there is public support for strong environmental regulations. The Bush campaign in 1988 recognized this by disassociating the Vice-President from the Reagan Administration's record in that area, trying to hearken back to Bush's record as a Texas Congressperson, and by attacking Governor Dukakis for

Table 3-3

Concern About the Environment, 1989 (in percent)

Worry About	A Great Deal	A Fair Amount	Only A Little	Not at All
Water Pollution	72	19	5	3
Toxic Waste	69	21	7	3
Air Pollution	63	25	8	4
Ocean and Beach Pollution	60	23	11	5
Loss of Natural Habitat	58	27	9	5
Damage to Ozone	51	26	13	8
Acid Rain	41	27	18	11
Greenhouse Effect	35	28	18	12

Rows may not sum to 100 percent because those saying they did not know are not included. Data are from *The Gallup Report*, June 1989, pp. 7–9.

the poor condition of Boston Harbor. Bush's claim that he "was an environmentalist" and the attacks on Dukakis were enough to diffuse the issue then. Still, the Republicans are vulnerable on this issue because of the opposition of business to stronger regulations. There is no reason the Democrats cannot use environmental issues, from local concerns with solid waste management and toxic waste to national concerns with acid rain and water and air pollution, to help build a progressive governing coalition.

Crime and Public Order

Issues of crime and public order are often problematic for the Democrats. Democrats (and liberals) are often seen as "soft on crime," too willing to "coddle criminals," and insensitive to victim's rights. But the crime issue is complicated and there are a number of ways the Democrats can appeal to the public in this area. First, and most importantly, is the area of drug abuse. Drugs are inextricably linked with crime. In a 1989 survey, Gallup found that 58 percent of the public felt drugs were the primary reason why crime had increased (in 1981 only 13 percent had named drugs as the primary culprit). This compared with only 4 percent who felt crime was on the rise because the courts were too lenient, and 4 percent who felt crime was on the increase because punishment of criminals was too lax.[22]

Thus, solving the drug program is, in many people's minds, a crucial element in fighting crime. And the public sees education as the number-one priority in fighting against drugs. Gallup found, for example, that 40 percent of the public felt our first priority in fighting drugs should be teaching about the dangers of drugs, compared with only 19 percent who felt our first priority should be arresting dealers and 4 percent who felt our first priority should be arresting drug users.[23] More Americans believe the best way to fight drugs and drug abuse is to reduce demand in the United States (48 percent) than believe the best way is to reduce the supply coming in from foreign countries (40 percent).[24] Democrats do not have to "change their views" on these issues to find broad public support.

Similarly, there is strong public support for tougher handgun control. The percentage of people preferring stricter handgun regulations has ranged between 60 percent and 70 percent since at least 1973 (with about 6 to 8 percent preferring looser restrictions and the rest wanting things the way they are now). Seventy-one percent of the public supports a complete ban on Saturday Night Specials, and 72 percent supports a complete ban on assault rifles.[25] The public does not support a ban on all handguns (in 1988, 59 percent opposed such action),[26] but it does, clearly, want more to be done in the way of gun control. In fact, Yeric and Todd, after summarizing public support for gun control and the lack of governmental action in that regard conclude that "the issue of lack of governmental response to gun registration demands by the pubic remains one of the more baffling questions in public opinion."[27]

There are, then, opportunities for progressive Democrats to discuss the issues of crime and public order without being on the defensive. Focusing on ending drug abuse and stricter gun control clearly fits with public perceptions of what needs to be done. In many ways, what is often important on the crime issue is the need to appear "tough." A candidate's stand on issues of crime and public order are often tied to his or her image as either tough or weak (which, as we saw in Chapter 2, is often crucial for voters who rely on a stylistic sense of politics). And Republicans have often used this issue to portray Democrats as weak.

The key issue here for the Republicans has been the death penalty. Liberal opposition to the death penalty is taken as a sign of weakness, and at least two-thirds of the public supports the death penalty.[28] Democrats who oppose the death penalty, however, do not have to fear that such opposition will guarantee them a weak image or prohibit their election. New York's Governor, Mario Cuomo, who has vetoed death penalty legislation in every year he has been governor, is the clearest example of this. Cuomo's strategy is to denounce the death penalty as wrong and move on to other crime issues. In particular, he offers an alternative of life imprisonment without parole to those whom others would condemn to death. He does not spend a lot of time explaining his opposition to the death penalty.

Arguments about whether the death penalty is an effective deterrent, or the racially biased way in which death penalty sentences are imposed, or the possibility of making a mistake simply focus attention on the issue and put opponents of the death penalty on the defensive. Public support for the death penalty is clear, long-standing, and unlikely to change. Arguing about it will not convince people to change their minds (just as Oliver North was never able to convince the public to change its view of aid to the Contras). What progressive opponents of the death penalty need to do, then, is not to change their view on the subject (this simply creates an image of a "wishy-washy" weak leader who changes his or her mind according to the latest polls) but to prevent the issue from becoming a test of character. Offering alternative "tough" measures to help stop crime (such as strict gun control legislation) is the best way to do that. In the long run, one may hope, as I do, that people can be convinced of the need to do away with the death penalty, but until that happens, liberal Democrats need to avoid allowing themselves to be distracted by that issue from discussing the multitude of policy issues on which the public supports progressive stands. Crime and public safety, then, need not be issues on which Democrats are constantly on the defensive.

Civil Rights and Women's Rights

Two other areas where liberals and Democrats often have an image problem are civil rights and women's rights. As noted earlier, 58 percent of the public feels that "sides too much with minorities" is a good or very good description of a liberal. And fully 69 percent of the public opposes Supreme Court rulings allowing for affirmative action programs.[29] Similarly, over 80 percent of the public prefers hiring "by merit" to giving preferential treatment to minorities or women.[30] Many people, then are skeptical of Democrats and liberals because they think they have gone too far in the area of equal rights. These people believe that affirmative action programs (or quotas) discriminate against others (in particular, white males) and are therefore unfair.

In a similar fashion, many citizens are skeptical of the activities of the women's movement. A February 1990 Gallup Poll found that 76 percent of the public believed the women's movement made it more difficult for marriages to succeed and 66 percent believed the women's movement made it more difficult for women to combine jobs and family.[31] When Walter Mondale was attacked in 1984 for being a captive of "special interests," to many people this meant he did "too much" for civil rights and women's rights groups.

On the other hand, there is strong public support for equal opportunities for blacks, Hispanics, women, and homosexuals. The same survey which found that people think the women's movement had made some things more difficult also found that 56 percent of the public feel that women do not have equal job opportunities. The 1988 American National Election Survey found that 69 percent of the public felt that men and women should have equal roles, with only 14 percent feeling a women's place is primarily in the home. And a July 1988 poll found that 73 percent of the public still supports the Equal Rights Amendment.[32] Similarly, more people think efforts to create equal opportunities for blacks and Hispanics have not gone far enough (40 and 46 percent respectively) than think such efforts have gone too far (39 percent and 28 percent).[33] Thirty-seven percent of the public feels we need to do more to integrate the schools compared with only 23 percent who feel we need to do less (31 percent feel current efforts are fine; 9 percent do not know).[34] And 71 percent of the public now believes that homosexuals should be given equal job opportunities (up from 59 percent in 1982).[35] Finally, 56 percent of the public feels private clubs should not be able to discriminate against women in choosing members (37 percent feel they should), and 78 percent feel such clubs should not be able to discriminate against blacks (18 percent feel they should have that right).[36]

The public, then, shows clear support for equality and equal rights for all citizens, and progressive Democrats should emphasize their support for such policies. The public is leery of what they see as attempts by some groups to gain an unfair advantage (affirmative action programs) and by some of what they see as the results of the women's movement. But the commitment to equality and justice is clear, and Democrats should feel no need to back down from that commitment. I do not want to underestimate the difficulties that racial tensions can create for the Democratic Party. Part of the problem results from the very different perceptions held by African-Americans and white Americans of the level of discrimination present in society, and I will return in Chapters 6 and 8 to a closer look at how these differences might be bridged. For now, however, we need to note that the public's commitment to equality has continued to increase.

Children's Issues: Child Care and Education

In contrast to civil rights and women's rights, there is little ambiguity among the public over issues relating to children. The public is strongly supportive of efforts by government to increase the quality of child care for preschool youngsters and the quality of education for school-age children. In terms of child care, Democratic pollster Stanley Greenberg stated: "We have not been able to find a way to word a child-care question that doesn't produce a positive response of over 60 percent."[37] And since figures indicate that in 1990 up to 80 percent of mothers with children under one year of age were working (the figure in 1988 was 52 percent),[38] this is an issue which is likely to continue to grow in importance.

Similarly, in July 1988, 66 percent of the public felt spending for education should be increased, and 64 percent of the public said it would pay higher taxes to raise educational standards. When asked to rank how important developing the best education system was in determining America's strength twenty-five years from now, 88 percent of the public said it was very important, compared with 65 percent who felt developing efficient industrial production was very important, and 47 percent who felt building the strongest military was very important.[39]

How we care for our children, then, is an issue of extreme importance to the American public. The public is strongly supportive of government activity to insure that our children are given quality education and care.

Abortion

Public opinion on the issue of abortion has been analyzed over and again since the 1989 *Webster* decision by the Supreme Court put the issue back into the political limelight. The public is clearly of two minds about abortion. It does not like abortion. (Fifty-seven percent agree that abortion is murder.) On the other hand, it feels women should be able to make their own decisions about whether to have an abortion. (Fifty-one percent agree with that statement).[40] Since the *Roe v. Wade* decision (which declared limits on the right to an abortion during the first trimester of pregnancy to be unconstitutional) in 1973, public opinion on

Table 3-4

Attitudes Toward Abortion, 1975–1991 (in percent)

Year	Should Always Be Legal	Should Sometimes Be Legal	Should Never Be Legal
1975	21	54	22
1977	22	55	19
1979	22	54	19
1980	25	53	18
1981	23	52	21
1983	23	58	16
1988	24	57	17
1990	31	53	12
1991	32	50	17

Data are from *The Gallup Poll Monthly*, April 1990, p. 3, and June 1991, p. 36. Rows may not sum to 100 percent because those expressing no opinion are not listed in the table.

the issue has hardly changed at all. There has been some movement in the pro-choice position in the period since 1988, but the predominant pattern is one of stability. As Table 3-4 indicates, most Americans do not like either extreme. They do not want to see abortion used as a method of birth control, but they do not want to see it eliminated as an option either. (Over 60 percent oppose the Supreme Court overturning the *Roe v. Wade* decision.)[41]

Still, abortion is more likely to be a problem for the Republicans than for the Democrats. First of all, the divisions in the Democratic Party on abortion, as William Schneider notes, have been present for quite some time. Most committed right-to-life activists have either left the party or come to terms with its position, since the right-to-life movement has been organizing to make political changes in abortion laws for over fifteen years. On the other hand, Republicans have never had to face their divisions squarely. As long as the courts protected the right to abortion in an unambiguous manner, the Republican Party could push the right-to-life position strongly without suffering major divisions. Since *Webster*, however, the restrictions that used to be theoretical are now real, and that forces pro-choice Republicans to examine their support for their party for the first time.

More importantly, the politics of the abortion issue make "compromise" positions more difficult for the Republican Party. The right-to-life movement supports a total ban on abortion (with the possible exception of when the physical life of the mother is threatened). Anything less is not acceptable. Right-to-lifers are likely, therefore, to be dissatisfied with any candidate who tries to forge a compromise on the issue. But the public clearly supports leaving the final decision about abortion up to the woman. It only wants women to exercise that option under certain conditions, but it clearly prefers having women make those decisions to having government make those decisions for them. Thus, pro-choice positions are more acceptable political solutions to the public than are right-to-life positions, even when the public shares some of the right-to-life movement's misgivings about the actual use of abortion.

The one exception to this is the issue of parental notification laws. Here the public does not support the pro-choice position, with 67 percent favoring parental consent laws.[42] In the minds of much of the public, minors are not capable of making these decisions for themselves. It is still not government that makes the choice; it is the parent (people do not support a ban on minors having abortion in the same way they support banning minors from buying alcohol—even if the minor's parents thought their child should buy alcohol). And the public is not likely to object to the enactment of such parental consent laws. On the other hand, a candidate who supports the right of a woman to make choices about abortion unless she is a minor is not likely to be acceptable to the right-to-life movement (and the right wing of the Republican Party), while a candidate who wants to restrict the rights of adult women to make choices about abortion along with the rights of minor women to have abortions without parental consent is not likely to be acceptable to a large proportion of the population, including a great many Republicans. Limiting the issue of abortion to the issue of parental consent, then, is not going to be easy, and abortion, therefore, is likely to be an issue which Republicans are not going to want to spend much time discussing over the next few years.

The "Values" Issue: Patriotism and Family

There is one other set of issues over which the Democrats often seem to fall on their collective faces: what we might call collectively the "values" issue. In the 1988 election, it was best represented by the Pledge of Allegiance controversy; and other topics include burning the American flag and school prayer. The liberal positions of not requiring the Pledge of Allegiance or school prayer and not amending the Constitution to prohibit flag burning are used to portray the Democrats as less patriotic or less committed to "traditional family values" than conservatives and/or Republicans. And it is clear that public opinion does overwhelmingly support the Republican/conservative positions of allowing school prayer, requiring the Pledge of Allegiance, and prohibiting flag burning. (For example, 70 percent of the public agreed with George Bush that the Pledge of Allegiance should be required in school).[43]

On the other hand, most people recognize that these issues in and of themselves are not that crucial. Two-thirds of the public, for example, felt the 1988 campaign should focus on "more important" issues than the Pledge of Allegiance.[44] But that does not mean progressive Democrats can ignore these questions or deal with them simply by arguing we should focus on other issues. Nor should Democrats dismiss these issues as unimportant. Rather, liberal Democrats need to recognize that these issues are symbolic of broader, very real concerns of many Americans. Jean Bethke Elshtain makes this case very clearly in her discussion of the 1988 election.[45] As she argues, these issues touch on a feeling (or fear) of many Americans that life in contemporary America is out of control and that we need to "return" to more traditional values such as patriotism and prayer to bring stability and renewed strength to America.

Liberal Democrats, therefore, need to recognize that these

fears and concerns are real, and they need to address them. Defending their views as patriotic (not legalistically as Michael Dukakis did) is one approach. Thus, for example, liberal Democrats can point to the fact that Russian citizens can now burn the Russian flag in Red Square as a sign of protest, laud Russia for the changes that allow this to be the case, and argue that American citizens should have that same right, even if we find the act offensive and insulting.

Additionally, progressive Democrats should not be embarrassed to talk about family, patriotism, or community. There is nothing inherently "conservative" about being patriotic or feeling good about your community. "Family" is not a Republican position.

In talking about these values, the Democrats need to do more than run slick commercials with lots of pictures of happy families and the American flag. Rather, they need to show how the policies they support will help revitalize families and communities and, therefore, help meet the concerns that are reflected in the public's positions on values issues. In the final chapter of the book, I will explore the kinds of policies the Democrats can use to help meet these and other public concerns. For now we simply need to note where the public stands on these issues and what that feeling reflects. As I pointed out in Chapter 2, public concern with images or symbolic issues usually is not simply an attraction to surface realities such as slick advertising or attractive packaging but rather reflects very deep feelings and very real attempts to sort out the meaning of a very complex and very distant political world.

Foreign Policy and National Defense

Finally, the area of foreign policy and national defense is also one which often hurts the Democrats. The party is seen as not being "tough enough" on these issues. One survey in October 1988, for example, found that 58 percent of the public felt George Bush would make U.S. defenses stronger, compared with only 12 percent who felt that way about Michael Dukakis.[46] Part

Table 3-5

Attitudes Toward Military Spending, 1969–1990 (in percent)

Year	Too Little	Just Right	Too Much	No Opinion
1969	8	31	52	9
1971	11	31	50	8
1973	13	30	46	11
1976	22	32	36	10
1981	51	22	15	12
1982	16	31	41	12
1983	21	36	37	6
1985	11	36	46	7
1986	13	36	47	4
1987	14	36	44	6
1988	17	42	35	6
1990	9	36	50	5

Data are from *The Gallup Poll Monthly*, January 1990, p. 10.

of this has to do with the "patriotism" issue discussed above. And liberal Democrats need to avoid the charge that they are "weak" on defense. But, again, in this area that does not mean they need to "move to the right." In fact, there is much public support for progressive foreign policy positions.

First of all, one of the ironies of the Reagan years is that the perceived success of Ronald Reagan in strengthening American defenses has caused a major decline in support for increased defense spending. As Table 3-5 shows, the percentage of the public thinking we spend too little on defense has declined from 51 to 9 and the percentage feeling we spend too much has grown from 15 to 50.[47]

Similarly, the 1988 American National Election Study found that 43 percent of the public felt cooperating with the Soviet Union was the best approach to take, while only 32 percent felt we needed to "get tough." And opposition to the deployment of the strategic defense initiative rose from 40 percent in 1986 to 50 percent in 1988.[48] The combination of these changes perceived to be brought on by the successes of the Reagan Administration with the rapidly changed situation in Eastern Europe and the former Soviet Union provides ample opportunity for the Democrats to push for a foreign policy more fully based on cooperation and negotiation and less focused on building a strong national defense. (Note too, the figures I cited in the section on children's issues, which indicate that people think education and economic development are more important for our long-term security than is a strong military defense.)

In addition, the public has shown reluctance to rely on military solutions to foreign policy problems. This can be seen most clearly in the steady opposition to military aid to the Contra rebels in Nicaragua that I discussed in Chapter 2. Even when faced with a question asking about helping the guerrillas to overthrow "the communist government in Nicaragua" (using the term "communism" maximizes public support for activity to defeat that government), 52 percent of the public said no. And after the Central American nations formulated their joint peace plan, 70 percent of the public felt the United States should wait and "give peace a chance" rather than continue aiding the Contras.[49] Opposition to military solutions can also be seen in the public's support (which reached 78 percent in 1984) for a verifiable freeze on the testing, production, and deployment of nuclear weapons.[50]

On the other hand, the successful conduct of the war in the Persian Gulf might be seen as a counter to this line of reasoning. Almost immediately after the war ended, Republicans began arguing that Democrats would need to "explain" their votes in opposition to that war. And the extraordinarily high approval ratings for President Bush's conduct of the war seem to confirm that analysis. (According to a *New York Times* survey done in the first week of March 1991, 83 percent of the public approved of the President's handling of foreign policy.)[51] But such an analysis overlooks an important factor. Public distaste for the use of force remains. Until the war began, there was strong support for continuing the use of sanctions and nonaggressive means of forcing Iraq out of Kuwait. Democrats can still legitimately argue that while they applaud the success of the war effort, they still felt their initial vote to delay action was the proper one. Furthermore, they can, and should, argue that the war was caused in part by the short-sighted policies of the Reagan and Bush Administrations, which encouraged Saddam Hussein and ignored his atrocities and his stockpiling of chemical weapons. In November 1990, for example, President Bush vetoed a bill which would have imposed sanctions on Iraq because of its use of chemical weapons.[52] If Democrats "need to answer for their opposition to the war," Republicans need to answer for their blindness to human rights which helped to encourage Saddam Hussein and make the war "necessary." If George Bush wants to make an issue of his conduct of the war in the Persian Gulf, the Democrats should not hesitate to remind people that our official policy, relayed to the Iraqis just a few days before they marched into Kuwait, was that we had no position on their border dispute with Kuwait, a position which clearly encouraged Saddam to invade. They also should make clear that for years the Bush and Reagan administrations overlooked the terrible atrocities going on in Iraq because of a short-sighted sense of our "national interest," which, in the end, made it necessary to risk American (and other) lives. The war may have been successful, but that does not mean it could not have been avoided. Given a choice between peace and war, the public is still likely to choose peace.

Nevertheless, the Persian Gulf crisis will increase the popularity of conservatives and Republicans, but more for the way it improves their "image" as strong and forceful, than because of a change in public attitudes about the use of force as a foreign policy tool that many pundits are describing. Progressive Democrats should not be afraid to argue that a more enlightened foreign policy, relying on diplomacy and collective action and not a broad military build-up, is the best way for the United States to pursue its goals.

Furthermore, the Persian Gulf crisis did not lead to blind support for everything President Bush has done. Far from it. As I noted in Chapter 2, the public is often more discriminating than we give it credit for. Support for Ronald Reagan did not translate into support for all of Ronald Reagan's policies, and support for the Persian Gulf has not caused the public to back away from the progressive policy positions noted earlier. Thus, that same *New York Times* survey which discerned overwhelming support for President Bush found that 68 percent of the public felt the Bush Administration has not shown enough concern for the homeless (compared with 21 percent who felt it had done enough), 62 percent felt the President had just talked about improving education (compared with 24 percent who felt he had made progress in that area), 53 percent felt the President had just talked about protecting the environment (compared with 35 percent who felt he had made progress in that area), and 52 percent felt he had just talked about the drug problem (compared with 38 percent who felt progress had been made).[53] The perceived successful conduct of Operation Desert Storm is not likely to make the American public any less receptive to a progressive political agenda, particularly on the domestic front but even in areas of foreign policy. And as the Persian Gulf War recedes into the past, the public will turn its attention more fully to domestic concerns and to new foreign policy issues such as how to deal with the revolutionary changes in Eastern Europe or bring peace to the Middle East. Progressive Democrats must not be afraid to argue that force should only be a course of last resort.

The other foreign policy attitude that Democrats and progressives can rely on is support for human rights and democracy abroad. This can be seen in public support for pressure on the South African government to end the practice of apartheid. In February 1990, for example, 38 percent of the public felt we should put more pressure on South Africa, 38 percent felt we should keep the same amount of pressure we currently use, and only 16 percent felt we should ease pressure.[54] Another example of this is public concern about the Intifada—uprising—of Palestinians demanding independence from Israel. For example, in spite of long-term American public support for Israel, in March of 1988 43 percent of the American public felt that Israel had been dealing too harshly with Palestinians involved in the Intifada; only 17 percent felt it was acting too leniently. And 30 percent of the public said Israel's actions had made them feel less favorable toward Israel. (Sixty percent said the actions left them with the same feelings toward Israel, and 5 percent said they felt better about Israel).[55] The point is not that progressive Democrats should argue for abandoning America's long-term commitment to Israel (a position the public also does not support). Rather, it is that the public is reluctant to support the use of force over the use of peaceful means to resolve disputes. In the Middle East, that means the public does not like Israel's reaction to the Intifada. But it also does not like the use of terrorist tactics by the Palestinians. An emphasis on nonviolent means of conflict resolution can, therefore, be the centerpiece of a "strong" American foreign policy.

The Democrats can draw on the public's desire for cooperation and peace, its concern with international economic security, and its concern for democracy and human rights abroad to build support for a progressive foreign policy agenda.

Conclusion

There is, then, strong support for liberal policy positions over a wide range of areas. It is true that liberals have an image problem, but that is something which can be dealt with through effective articulation of liberal philosophy. Similarly, there are issues (such as the death penalty) where the public does not support traditional liberal views. But, again, that is not an insurmountable problem. The raw materials are clearly present to build a governing coalition supportive of basic progressive policies. The public does support such positions. Democrats do not have to "move to the right" in order to convince the public to support their views. One of the ironies of the Reagan years is that eight years of conservative government did not make the public more supportive of conservative policy positions. The public never agreed with Ronald Reagan's political philosophy, even when it voted for him in 1980 and 1984. In 1980 it did not like the state of the economy under Jimmy Carter, and in 1984 the public was expressing satisfaction with two years of economic growth, but there never was any evidence they were supporting an across-the-board conservative mandate.[56] The Democrats need to remember that. The public will support a progressive political agenda.

Three things stand in the way of progressive success at such an endeavor. One is the skepticism and distrust people have of government. They like the idea of government being active to help improve our society, but they become fearful that any concrete program we implement will become riddled with waste, fraud, and corruption. Hence, they hesitate to support overly activist policies.

Second is the negative image many people have of liberals and Democrats. In many ways, this image is tied to the distrust of government noted above. But as I outlined at the beginning of this chapter, it does go beyond that. People do not feel as comfortable with "liberals" running things as they do with "conservatives" in charge.

And third, there is the issue of taxes. Active government is expensive. Democrats need to be able to answer the question of how they are going to pay for the programs they want to implement, particularly in this era of multibillion dollar deficits. In the final chapter of the book, I hope to show how the Democrats can offer a progressive platform which can both rebuild public trust in government and rebuild the image of liberals (or at least negate their negative image). But now we need to turn our attention to taxes and what the public really thinks about that issue.

4

"Read My Lips": The Myths about Public Attitudes on Taxes

". . . and I'll say, 'Read my lips. *No new taxes.*' "
—George Bush

Conventional wisdom in American politics in the late 1980s and early 1990s tells us that the public is unalterably opposed to raising taxes. George Bush's promise never to raise taxes is cited as one reason why he was elected President in 1988, and Walter Mondale's promise to raise taxes is blamed for the size of his defeat in the presidential election of 1984. But as is often the case, the conventional wisdom is only partially true. The public does not like the prospect of higher taxes (and why should they?), but they are not unalterably opposed to them either. It is not taxes that people dislike, but the tax system and the government that is administering it. As we shall see, the actual views of citizens on tax issues are more complex and more ambivalent than the conventional wisdom would have us believe. Evidence from both public opinion surveys and the results of citizen initiatives and referendums show a public willing to accept (and even support) higher taxes under the proper circumstances.

Table 4-1

Attitudes Toward Taxing and Spending, 1989 (in percent)

	Support More Spending	Will Pay More Taxes	Will Pay $100/year More in Taxes
Education	76	63	59
Drugs	75	57	56
The Homeless	71	58	59
Health Care	67	57	52
Pollution	59	36	34
AIDS	59	36	34
Job Training	56	40	30
Help Low-Income Families	56	40	30
Aid Farmers	48	38	31
Health Insurance	48	38	31
Aid College Students	44	32	27
Childcare	41	29	28
First-time Home Buyers	37	25	21
Space Exploration	21	13	13
Defense Spending	14	10	11

Data come from *The Gallup Report*, October 1989, p. 6.

Public Opinion on Tax Issues

The public does not always oppose tax increases. In fact, the public expresses a willingness to pay more in taxes for a wide variety of programs. For example, a 1989 Gallup survey found over half the public was willing to pay $100 a year more in taxes in order to increase spending on public education, drugs, helping the homeless, and health care, and over one-third were also willing to pay that much more for cleaning up environmental pollution, more AIDS research, helping low income families, and aiding farmers.[1] (See Table 4-1.)

Similarly, 75 percent of the public support a higher tax on alcohol to reduce the deficit, and 71 percent of the public support a higher tax on cigarettes to achieve that goal.

On the other hand, only 29 percent support a national sales tax for deficit reduction and an even smaller 15 percent support a rise

Table 4-2

Support for Taxes to Solve Social Problems, 1988 (in percent)

Problem	Not a Problem	No Gov't. Action Needed	Needs Gov't. Action, But No New Taxes	Needs Gov't. Action Even with New Taxes	Don't Know
Halt drug smuggling	2	6	24	66	2
Decent standard of living for elderly	2	11	29	56	2
Adequate medical care	2	13	32	51	2
Improve public education	5	20	26	47	2
Provide health insurance	4	17	32	45	2
Ensure all can read and write	5	27	25	40	3
Ensure all have a place to sleep and eat	4	23	32	39	2
Ensure equal opportunities for jobs	8	29	37	23	3
Provide jobs for all	8	34	33	23	2
Protect workers from sudden layoffs	6	35	34	18	7
Ensure all can send children to college	13	39	27	18	3
Ensure quality of TV improves	33	45	13	6	3

Data are from a survey done for the *Times Mirror* in May 1988 by the Gallup Organization and reported in *Public Opinion*, March/April 1989, p. 21.

in income taxes to help solve the deficit problem.[2] A more general question asked by Gallup found that 68 percent of the public opposed tax increases to reduce the deficit.[3] The deficit is not a problem which the public wants to pay more money to solve. And that is not surprising. Unlike improving education or fighting drugs, programs that hold out concrete benefits which citizens can relate to, solving the deficit offers only the more abstract (though not necessarily less important) reward of putting the country's finances in better order.

As noted in Chapter 3, the public does support government activity in many areas. And people maintain that support even if they think it is going to mean more in government taxes. But the public is selective in that regard. Table 4-2 reinforces that conclusion.[4]

Some activities are worth spending more money on, others are not. Individuals have different mixes of programs which they support. In a study of these attitudes in 1980 and 1982, for example, I found that while the average citizen cited more programs they wanted to increase than decrease, very few citizens want to increase spending in all areas. Most saw some areas where they felt spending could go up, and others where spending needed to (or could) decline. For many citizens, then, the way to increase spending in areas they support without raising taxes is to decrease spending in those areas where they think money is being wasted or put to improper uses.[5]

One result of this pattern is that the public is often unfairly blamed for irrationality. The public wants higher spending, but is blamed for not wanting to pay the price. But this "public irrationality" may, in fact, reflect the way we aggregate these opinions. Individuals may be completely rational, feeling that cuts in "bad" programs can compensate for the increases they desire. But when we add up different people's views of where to cut and where to increase, we are left with more programs to increase than cuts to be found. But that is a very different political problem from the problem of individuals wanting "something for nothing." There is little evidence that individual citizens actually want something for nothing. Most recognize that increased spending will require increased taxes or decreased spending somewhere else. The opposition to higher taxes that does arise is not, then, simply a refusal to pay more. In fact, in some areas the public is clearly willing to pay more. Dissatisfaction with taxes springs from two other sources.

The first source of public dissatisfaction with taxes is the perception that the government wastes a lot of money. A 1988 Gallup survey found that 71 percent of the public felt the government "wastes a lot of tax dollars," and another 24 percent felt the government "wastes some tax dollars." [6] Given that feeling, it is not surprising that many people feel we can spend more in a number of areas without increasing taxes. If the government is wasting enormous sums of money, all we need to do is cut out waste and spend our money more efficiently. Increasing taxes, in this view, will only increase waste.

This, in turn, feeds into the problem for the Democrats I cited earlier. People want the government to do things in the abstract, but when they think about actually having government do things in practice, they are much more skeptical. A 1986 CBS/*New York Times* poll, for example, found that 62 percent of the public agreed with the statement that in general "the federal government creates more problems than it solves." [7] And in the area of taxing and spending, that problem is clearly one of waste. As long as the public views the government as overly wasteful, Democratic proposals to increase funding to pay for the things which people want will face strong opposition. Restoring faith in government is a major obstacle to progressive politics.

The second factor in public opposition to taxes is the perception that the tax system is unfair. The public objects not to their absolute level of taxation, but to their perceived relative level of taxation. The problem is that the tax system is seen as riddled with loopholes and regulations which help the rich, while the middle class is stuck paying more than their fair share. This is not surprising. In fact, even without looking at the issue of loopholes and deductions, the top tax rate for individuals with over $100,000 in income drops down below that for individuals earning $50,000. That people might see this as unfair should come as no shock. And in July 1988, a CBS/*New York Times* survey found that 63 percent of the public favored increasing the tax rates for those making over $100,000 dollars a year.

The first campaign pledge I would recommend that Democrats give, then, is to make the tax system fairer, and I would begin with a promise to make the richest American families pay at least the same tax rate (if not a higher tax rate) than Americans earning less money. It is inconceivable that the Republicans have much to gain politically by trying to defend lower rates for richer people. But if they go along with this change, they alienate their most committed anti-tax supporters as well as higher income Republicans.

But fairness in taxes goes beyond this simple change. Public perception of the Tax Reform Act of 1986 is that, far from improving the situation, it simply made things worse. A March 1990 Gallup poll found that only 9 percent of the public felt tax reform had made for a fairer sharing of the tax burden, while 37 percent felt it had made things less fair, and 40 percent felt it made no difference. Similarly, only 12 percent felt the reforms had made the tax system simpler, while 31 percent felt it had made things more complicated, and 48 percent felt it had made no difference in that regard. And 56 percent felt that reform had led to an increase in taxes, while only 7 percent felt their taxes had gone down.[8]

The real issue in the "tax revolt," then, is not how much people are paying (though that clearly plays a role), but the perception that others are not paying their fair share. My in-depth interviews found this to be a widespread feeling as well. For example, John, a middle-class salesperson, argued:

> If I was upper class, I would think the tax system was fair. Okay, I really don't think your upper-class people should get taxed on the same sense as the middle- or the lower middle-class people. It seems to be they got the money, and there's too many loopholes where they can put the money and no taxation.[9]

The issue for the Democrats, then, should not be "taxes" but "fair taxes." Victor Fingerhut, a Democratic Party pollster and consultant, once said to me that Walter Mondale's mistake in

1984 was not saying he would raise taxes, but that he did not add "for the rich" to that phrase. Public attitudes on tax issues seem to support that view. The Democrats can talk about taxes and revenues and changing the system, but they need to do so in the context of supporting the kinds of programs that people see as important and in the context of creating a tax system where the wealthy pay their fair share of the burden. When people are asked which is the worst tax (given a choice of the federal income tax, the state income tax, state sales tax, and local property taxes), a third of the public choose the federal income tax and a little over a quarter (28 percent) choose the local property tax, while only 18 percent and 10 percent choose the state sales and income taxes respectively.[10] The Democrats need to offer tax policies that attack this perception of unfairness in the tax structure.

On the other hand, opponents of tax increases often say that public opinion surveys are misleading on this issue. According to this view, people say they will support higher taxes, but when push comes to shove, they do not. And as evidence they point to citizen support for strong tax-cutting measures, beginning with the passage of Proposition 13 in California in June 1978. But the record of such tax measures is far from clear. In fact, the "tax revolt" may be as much myth as reality. We need to turn, then, to the actual record of tax-related initiatives and referendums.

Tax-Related Initiatives and Referendums

On June 6, 1978, California voters passed Proposition 13 by a two to one margin. This action sharply reduced property taxes in California and was heralded as the beginning of the "tax revolt."[11] California voters were angry at the substantial rise in property taxes been fueled by the real estate boom, especially in Southern California. This boom had seen dramatic increases in real estate values, and, therefore, in property taxes, but to most homeowners, the boom was largely abstract. The value of their home and their tax burden was rising, but they were not taking home any more pay to cover the costs of that increase. Voter initiatives similar to Proposition 13 had lost on two previous occasions, but by June 1978 Californians had had enough. The tax revolt had begun. Politics in California and the rest of the nation began to reflect the growing belief that voters would not tolerate new taxes. As we have seen, public opinion surveys indicate that that view is as much myth as reality. Voter responses to initiatives and referendum dealing with taxes reflect that conclusion as well.

Almost as soon as the ink had dried on Proposition 13, the public began showing that its views on taxes were more complex than the supporters of the tax revolt indicated. The headline in the *Washington Post* on November 9, 1978 read: "Proposition 13 Aftermath: A Tax Revolt That Didn't Happen."[12] Of the eight states voting on proposals to limit state and local taxes in some way, five (Idaho, Missouri, Nevada, North Dakota, and Texas) followed California's lead, while three states (Arkansas, Michigan, and Oregon) rejected such propositions. Proposals to limit state spending were more successful, passing in six states and failing in only one (though one of the six was Michigan, which, as noted, had rejected a tax cut proposition). Montgomery County, Virginia, defeated a tax cut proposition, while neighboring Prince George County passed a one-year freeze on county spending.

In 1979, California voters gave more impetus to the tax revolt by passing Proposition 4, which limited the amount of spending the government could undertake without receiving voter approval. Voters in Washington state passed a proposition which limited the growth rates of both government spending and taxes. On the other hand, Oklahoma voters defeated a proposition which would have put a lid of 6 percent on the state income tax (at the time, the top bracket was 17 percent), a vote which, according to the *Christian Science Monitor*, was "a surprise even to opponents of the measure who were predicting it would pass."[13]

In many ways, 1980 was the high point of the tax revolt. Election day 1980 saw thirty-seven tax-related ballot questions in eighteen states. And Massachusetts voters, fueled by the same

Table 4-3

Results from Statewide Taxation and Spending Limit Propositions

Year	Liberal Victories		Conservative Victories	
1978	7	(6)	14	(13)
1979	1	(1)	2	(2)
1980	17	(8)	21	(11)
1981	1	(1)	3	(3)
1982	3	(3)	12	(9)
1983	3	(2)	0	(0)
1984	7	(6)	1	(1)
1985	0	(0)	1	(1)
1986	4	(4)	6	(4)
1987	0	(0)	1	(1)
1988	8	(6)	3	(3)
1989	4	(2)	8	(5)
1990	6	(6)	1	(1)

Numbers in parentheses are the number of states with liberal or conservative results. (Some states had more than one proposition in a single year. In cases where voters rejected a more conservative proposition for a milder one, the state result was counted as liberal. If a state split in its results, one conservative victory and one liberal victory, without the two propositions competing such that passage of one would have made passage of the other redundant, it was counted in both columns.)

kind of anger over property tax hikes resulting from a boom in real estate values that had led to Proposition 13, passed what became known as Proposition 2 1/2. This, in the "liberal" state of Massachusetts, seemed to confirm the widespread and "almost universal" appeal of the tax revolt. But again, a closer look shows a more mixed picture. Twenty of the thirty-seven tax propositions on the ballot in November 1980 passed, but many of them were relatively noncontroversial tax exemptions for the elderly and/or disabled. (Such tax exemptions, for example, passed in New Jersey, Louisiana, West Virginia, and Virginia). On the other hand, many of the seventeen propositions which went down to defeat were more far-reaching Proposition 13–style tax cuts. (Such measures failed in South Dakota, Arizona, Nevada, Oregon, Utah, and Michigan—in fact, Michigan voters defeated three different tax cut propositions). And California voters defeated an initiative sponsored by Howard Jarvis, the author of Proposition 13, that would have cut the state income tax in half. Of the more extensive tax reduction propositions, only Arkansas and the widely heralded Massachusetts propositions passed. In addition, a "progressive" tax reform proposition in Ohio, which would have cut property taxes but simultaneously increased taxes for the rich and for banks and other businesses, was defeated. The *Washington Post* headline after the election again summed up the general state of affairs: "Most Tax Overhaul Measures are Defeated."[14]

Thus, the record of tax-cutting initiatives and referendums since the beginning of the tax revolt in 1978 has been decidedly mixed. Some have passed, but some have failed. Table 4-3 summarizes the results in statewide tax and spending related propositions since 1978. (It does not, however, include bonding issues). As the table indicates, neither the number of conservative nor liberal victories is overwhelming. (The "progressive" Ohio property tax cut proposition and any other proposition which tied one type of tax cut to increases in more progressive taxes are counted as liberal, not conservative propositions. Any proposition which simply cut taxes or limited government spending is counted as a conservative proposition.)[15] By my count, in the period between 1978 and 1989, there was a total of 127 statewide tax-related propositions: in 72 of them (57 percent), there was a conservative outcome, and in 55 (43 percent) a liberal outcome.

In addition, most of the liberal or conservative "victories" have been relatively minor. As in 1980, the most drastic measures either to cut or raise taxes have usually been defeated. Milder measures involving tax exemptions for certain kinds of people (such as veterans or the physically disabled) or certain kinds of products (such as household goods)—which I have counted as conservative victories—are the most likely to pass. Similarly citizens have been more willing to support minor increases in sales or gasoline taxes than to support major changes in the tax burden. Summing up an October 1989 Louisiana vote in which citizens supported a rise in the gasoline tax but rejected increased property taxes, Edward Renwick, a political analyst, commented: "Basically, people said we'll give you a little money if you use it for specific purposes."[16]

There have, in fact, been far fewer attempts actually to raise taxes by popular vote. The most visible of these was the recent successful June 1990 vote in California to double the gasoline tax in order to raise money for mass transit, schools, and poverty programs. That vote prompted conservative economist Arthur Laffer to bemoan the fact that it "really does end the tax revolt in California." And Democratic Assembly Speaker Willie Brown commented, "I believe it [the vote] clearly says if you come with a good reason to spend the money, voters will approve and sanction what you've done."[17]

Earlier, in 1988, voters in California voted to increase the cigarette tax by 25 cents per pack, and in October 1989, as just noted, Louisiana voters passed a measure raising the gasoline tax. On the other hand, in that same Louisiana vote, voters defeated a proposal to allow municipal governments to increase the property tax, and in May 1989, Pennsylvania voters rejected a plan to increase the state income taxes in return for lower property taxes.[18]

Results from local elections show the same kind of ambivalence. At times voters support increased taxes or oppose reduced taxes. For example, voters in Cleveland supported a 1-to–1.5 percent tax increase in February 1979 to help the city out of financial difficulties, Detroit voters approved an income tax increase of 1 percent in June 1981, and Kansas City voters approved a one-quarter of a cent hike in the sales tax to finance the war on drugs in 1989. On the other hand, New Orleans voters rejected a property tax increase in 1987 to pay for more police and fire protection, and St. Louis voters rejected a plan in 1989 to raise property taxes in order to fund the local symphony orchestra.[19]

The pattern of voter response to taxing and spending propositions mirrors the results of public opinion surveys. Citizens do not like higher taxes, but they are not unalterably opposed to them either. In fact, if they think it is for a worthwhile cause, they will support higher taxes, both theoretically in response to a survey question and practically by voting for propositions which will raise taxes. Of course, the high levels of dissatisfaction with government and the perception of massive waste in the federal budget lead to a great deal of skepticism about higher taxes. People worry that the money they want to spend on "worthy" projects will end up financing some kind of boondoggle, such as the infamous $75 replacement screws used at the Pentagon. Furthermore, there is widespread sentiment that the tax system is not fair, which leads to further resistance to tax increases since the feeling is that so many other (especially rich) people are not paying their "fair share."

Thus, while the Democrats should not be afraid to broach the subject of new taxes, they do need to recognize the actual sources of public resistance in that area. Pushing for a fairer tax structure is one way to deal with the problem. But the most important way, again, is to rebuild public trust in government. If people think they are getting their money's worth, they will support the kinds of progressive policies the Democrats have to offer. But if they think government is more problem than solution, then they will be attracted to Republican cries that "tax and spend" Democrats are "running the country into the ground." A 1985 Gallup survey found, when given a choice among big government, big business, and big labor, 50 percent of the public thought that big government was the major threat to the country's well-being, while only 22 percent chose big business and 19 percent chose big labor.[20] Rebuilding the ties that people have with their government is absolutely necessary for the long-term health of progressive politics and the Democratic Party.

Conclusion to Part One

The myths about public opinion in the United States in the 1990s tell us that we elect people based on their television appeal, that the public has come to support the conservative agenda of Ronald Reagan and George Bush, and that the public will not accept new taxes. In fact, a closer look at the evidence has shown us:

(1) Political "style" does matter, but in the end, policy (or political realities) will win out. Many members of the public do
judge political figures by their styles. They look for leaders
who will be tough or compassionate or honest (or all three).
And, thus, "image" does matter. But it is wrong, very wrong,
to conclude that image is *all* that matters. In fact, for many,
style is a way to predict performance. The public often finds
it difficult to know what policies will work best, and they feel
most comfortable making judgments about things based on
their own experiences. They know which kind of people are
successful. They have had experience with good and bad
bosses and workers. And they, therefore, look for the kinds of
qualities in their leaders which they think will lead to success.

However, since it is impossible to know whether George
Bush is actually "tough enough" or "compassionate enough"
or "honest enough," such voters rely heavily on retrospective
evaluations. If things are going well, they made the right
decision in choosing a leader. If not, they misjudged the character of the leader they elected. The pattern of Ronald
Reagan's performance ratings reflects this fact. It is not
enough to look good on television. Solid, effective policies
are what matter most.

(2) The public is supportive of a broad range of progressive policies. Public opinion surveys are clear in that regard. And
public opinion on these matters has not shifted much as a
result of eight years of President Reagan and three years of
President Bush. People supported Ronald Reagan because
they felt his administration kept the economy in reasonably
good working order, not because they agreed with his political philosophy. As a result, there is opportunity to elect an
administration committed to a progressive platform. In fact,
such a platform is relatively attractive to the public. The
Democrats do not have to abandon liberal or progressive pol-

icies to win popular support. They do need to convince the public that they are capable of governing. But adopting more conservative policy positions is not the way to do that. (In fact, that is likely to reinforce the Democrats' image as "wishy-washy liberals who can't make up their minds.") The public may be "stylistically conservative," but it is still "operationally liberal." And the Democrats should try to draw on that policy support.

(3) The public is not unalterably opposed to new taxes. It will support tax increases or oppose tax cuts if it feels its money is not being wasted and the revenues are necessary for important government programs. In addition, there is widespread sentiment that the tax system is unfair.

4) People do not trust the government. The major problem with building a progressive coalition is that people do not trust the government to do the things they would like it to do. The public feels alienated and disconnected from the government in Washington, and this leads to skepticism about governmental solutions to the problems people see.

In the end, then, this look at the public indicates that the task for progressive Democrats is two-fold. First, the Democrats need to overcome the "image" problems that they have. In order for a Democrat to win the White House, they need to show that they are as likely as Republicans to be effective leaders. (A July 1991 CBS/*New York Times* survey found that 57 percent of the public said the Republicans are the party that provides better presidential candidates. Only 26 percent picked the Democrats. The rest saw no difference.)[21] This does not, I hope to show, involve running slick media campaigns high on style but short on issues. (In fact, one of Michael Dukakis's fatal mistakes, I would argue, was to think he would win the 1988 election if he could make it a referendum on "competence"—that is, style—rather than ideology—that is, ideas and policies.) The Democrats do need to be attentive to these matters. Ignoring them will not make them go away. But the best way to deal with them is by beginning with the Democrat's strength: the general level of support that exists for progressive policies in a wide range of areas. By itself, this level of support will not solve the problem, but it is the place where the Democrats can begin to appeal to the public and build a progressive coalition.

Second, the Democrats need to rebuild public confidence in government. They need to convince the public that government can be an instrument which carries out society's collective wishes. They need people to feel that government is working for them and with them, not against them. They need for people to feel connected with government. In the long run, progressive politics depends on such feelings. If the Democrats were to win a Presidential election based on a slick media campaign that changed their "image" without addressing this problem, it would be a hollow victory. Without change in this area, public support for government programs to address our needs in fields such as education, tax reform, the environment, poverty, and health care would be lacking. Progressive government requires public support.

Building a progressive coalition cannot, therefore, be accomplished in a single election. Even if the Democrats were to win in 1992 based on dissatisfaction with the state of the country under George Bush, they would still need to address these long-term trends in order to reinvigorate the nation in a progressive direction. Reconnecting the public to government is a slow, long-term process, but it is clearly one to which the public is open. In the long run, if the Democrats can develop lines of trust and communication between citizens and government and make citizens feel a part of their own government, then they can usher in another era of progressive government. If they win the White House but fail to use that opportunity to build such ties, their victory will a pyrrhic one for progressive politics, one filled with frustration and continued public skepticism.

In Part Three of this book, I will outline the kinds of policies which can, I believe, help reconnect the public to its government and build a Democratic Party committed to and able to implement progressive policies. Such policies, I will argue, will also help address the "image" problems that the Democrats face. But before we turn to those policies, we need to take a look at the party coalitions. One way to explore public opinion, as we have just done, is to look at the issues and concerns that seem to motivate people. But another important way to view these matters is to examine the groups that are most (or least) likely to support a progressive coalition. Where, in effect, will the Democrats votes come from? And more importantly, what are the issues which tend to pull potential Democrats (or Republicans) together? And what are the issues which tend to pull the Democratic (or Republican) coalition apart? We need to understand these matters before we can fully understand the best way to rebuild the Democratic Party.

Part Two

Party Coalitions in the 1990s

5

The Myth of a Republican "Lock" on the Electoral College

In Part One, we saw that the raw materials exist to build a progressive Democratic Party. The public does, in fact, support a wide range of progressive policy options and the Democrats can, therefore, tap into that desire in order to rebuild themselves. In this section of the book, we will look more closely at where the votes are. Rebuilding a reliable Democratic majority requires putting together a coalition of voters. In Chapters 6 and 7 we will explore this issue by focusing on voters as members of particular demographic groups and on the forces which pull together (and pull apart) the Democratic and Republican coalitions. But first, I want to explore the geographic make-up of the Democrat's potential constituency. As Part Three will make clear, while I firmly believe that the Democrats' strategy for building a long-term governing majority must focus to a large extent on local issues and concerns, it is also important that the Democrats be able to elect a progressive President. The leadership that such an individual can provide in leading the country and the party to adopt more progressive policies cannot be overstated. But one of the difficulties facing liberal Democrats is the widespread belief that it is practically impossible for a liberal Democrat to assem-

Table 5-1

The Republican "Lock" on the Electoral College

States Won by the Republicans Since 1968

State	Electoral Votes		State	Electoral Votes	
	1988	1992		1988	1992
Alaska	3	3	New Hampshire	4	4
Arizona	7	8	New Jersey	16	15
California	47	54	New Mexico	5	5
Colorado	8	8	North Dakota	3	3
Idaho	4	4	Oklahoma	8	8
Illinois	24	22	South Dakota	3	3
Indiana	12	12	Utah	5	5
Kansas	7	6	Vermont	3	3
Montana	4	3	Virginia	12	13
Nebraska	5	5	Wyoming	3	3
Nevada	4	4	TOTAL	187	191

States Won by the Republicans Since 1972

	Electoral Votes			Electoral Votes	
Connecticut	8	8	Michigan	20	18
Maine	4	4	TOTAL	32	30

ble a majority in the electoral college. That belief, I hope to show, is unfounded.

Republican Dominance of the Electoral College, 1968–1988

The Republican Party's victories in five of the past six presidential elections, combined with the continuing growth of the more Republican parts of the nation and the relative population decline of the more Democratic sections of the country, have led some to argue that the Republican Party's hold on the electoral college is secure. In early October 1988, for example, Republican strategist Lee Atwater said that the Bush campaign was confident that it had over 200 electoral votes locked up.[1] Furthermore, this argument goes, if the Democrats are to win, they need to win a number of states in the South, particularly Texas, and to win in these states a more moderate or conservative Democratic Party is necessary.

On the surface, this argument seems compelling. There are 21 states that the Democrats have lost in every election after the Johnson landslide in 1964. (See Table 5-1.) These include a number of large states such as California, Illinois, and New Jersey and in 1988 accounted for 187 electoral votes. Furthermore, there are 3 states, Connecticut, Maine and Michigan, which the Republicans have carried in every election since 1968. In 1988, these 3 states accounted for an additional 32 electoral votes. These 24 states, then, provided George Bush with 219 of the 270 electoral votes needed for an electoral college majority. In addition, there are a large number of southern states that Jimmy Carter carried in 1976 which seem very safely Republican. Arkansas, Kentucky, North Carolina, South Carolina, Tennessee, Florida, Texas, Alabama, and Mississippi all supported Jimmy Carter in 1976 but reverted to the Republican column in 1980. They account for an additional 110 electoral votes. And Georgia, the only southern state to remain loyal to Jimmy Carter in 1980, accounted for another 12. When you add these southern votes to the first 219, you have a total of 341 electoral votes for George Bush in 1988, more than enough to win the election. Michael Dukakis could have won every other state in the country, and he still would have been well short of the necessary 270 electoral votes.

Supporters of this theory, such as the Democratic Leadership Council, a group of mostly southern and mostly moderate-to-conservative Democrats, go on to note that the one Democratic victory in this time was Jimmy Carter's 1976 victory. Carter, they note, was able to carry much of the South, and that allowed him to defeat Gerald Ford. The recommendation they make is that the Democrats move away from, in the words of Charles Robb of Virginia, a former Chair of the Council: "the programmatic rigidity of what some have called liberal fundamentalism." Robb and others call for a "mainstream revolt against the orthodoxies and litmus tests that divide our party and stifle its political imagination."[2] This "mainstream revolt" involves moving the party "back to the center" and away from the kind of progressive politics I am recommending here. Such a move, the theory goes, will allow the Democrats to recapture the South and, therefore, win a majority in the electoral college.

In addition, the 1990 census is, according to this view, going to make such a strategy even more profitable. The states which made up the list of 219 electoral votes the Democrats have not carried since 1968 will increase to 221 electoral votes for 1992. (California alone will increase by 7 votes, but the net loss in the other 23 states is 5.) Similarly, the 10 states in the South that Jimmy Carter did carry (he never carried Virginia), will gain an additional 7 electoral votes. Florida will pick up 4 seats, and Texas will gain 3. North Carolina and Georgia each will gain single seats, but Kentucky and Louisiana are each losing one. Still, this brings the "safe" Republican total in 1992 up to 350 seats.[3] The task for the Democrats, in fact, seems daunting. But are these states that have consistently voted Republican really safe for the Republicans? A close look at statewide elections in these states yields a very different answer from what one gets from this examination of electoral vote totals. Clearly, presidential elections are different from gubernatorial and senatorial elections. Voters may not be looking for exactly the same thing. On the other hand, looking at the successes of progressive Democrats at lower levels of office does tell us something about the potential for candidates with progressive platforms and records to win elections. There is no easy translation of votes from one office to another, but there is no reason to believe that an electorate willing to support a progressive Democrat for statewide office would not be willing to support such a candidate for President.

Building A Democratic Majority I: The Core

In the 1988 presidential election, Michael Dukakis carried ten states and the District of Columbia with an electoral vote total of 112. Geographically, the states basically fell into three areas. First, there were three states in the Northeast, New York, Massachusetts, and Rhode Island. Second, there were three states in the upper Midwest, Wisconsin, Iowa, and Minnesota. And third, there were three states in the Pacific Rim, Oregon, Washington, and Hawaii. The tenth state was West Virginia. These states make up the core of any liberal Democratic coalition.

None of these states, it seems, is a "fluke." Massachusetts is the home state of Governor Dukakis, but it also has elected two of the most liberal members of the United States Senate, Ted Kennedy and John Kerry, and has an almost uniformly liberal Democratic House delegation. Even a non-Massachusetts liberal Democratic could feel that this state was relatively safe in his or her column.[4]

The other states that Dukakis carried show a similar pattern. They consistently elect liberal Democrats to statewide office (for example, Tom Harkin in Iowa, Paul Wellstone in Minnesota, and Mario Cuomo in New York) and are places where any liberal Democrat would make a strong candidate. It is true that environmental and "social" issues seem more important to the liberalism of the Pacific Rim states, while economic liberalism is more central in the midwestern states (and West Virginia), with the northeastern states seeming to fall somewhere in between. But all of these states have progressive bases which are strong enough to form the core geographic base of a liberal Democratic majority. Unfortunately, the only one of these states gain an electoral vote in 1992 is Washington, while four of them, Massachusetts, Iowa, West Virginia, and New York, will lose seats (the former three each will lose a single seat, while New York will lose three seats). Thus, in 1992, these core states will account for 107 electoral votes.

Building a Democratic Majority II:
The Northeast, Midwest, and California

There are a number of states in the Northeast and Midwest which George Bush carried in 1988 that are clearly amenable to liberal, progressive politics. These states, plus California, form the second part of a progressive coalition. The 1988 election results signal they are not as safe as those states Dukakis carried, but their politics and election results do indicate that liberal, progressive Democrats can, and do, win statewide elections in these states.

The Northeast

Three of these states, Maine, Vermont, and Connecticut, are in New England. In 1988, these states accounted for 11 electoral votes, a number which will remain the same in 1992.

The Democrats last carried Maine in a presidential election in 1968, and George Bush won a comfortable 55 percent of the vote there in 1988. Still, Bush's showing may overstate the strength of the Republican Party in Maine. First, Bush is a part-time resident of Maine. He may claim to be a Texas resident. But Bush actually does spend time in Maine, unlike his Texas residency. His family compound in Kennebunkport is a frequent vacation spot, and Bush has always had a fair amount of visibility there. Thus, in some ways, Bush had a "home state advantage" in Maine. In addition, at the same time Maine voters were supporting Bush, they also were reelecting Senate Majority Leader George Mitchell (who was running, basically, unopposed—his opponent was a conservative activist with little financial support) with 81 percent of the vote. And Mitchell, clearly, is a liberal. His Americans for Democratic Action (ADA) rating in both 1987 and 1988, the two years prior to his reelection, was 95.[5] In 1989 and 1990, they were 80 and 83. Similarly, Joseph Brennan, who represented one of Maine's two congressional districts, had ADA ratings of 95 and 89 in 1989 and 1990 respectively, and Maine's other representative, Republican Olympia Snowe, is a moderate Republican. Brennan gave up his seat to run for governor in 1990, when he was narrowly defeated (47 percent to 44) by Republican incumbent John McKernan, but he was replaced by a progressive Democrat, Thomas Andrews, who easily defeated a conservative Republican (and former Representative), Joseph Emery.[6]

The politics of Vermont has changed greatly over the past twenty years. Once one of the safest Republican states in the country, mirroring its next door neighbor, New Hampshire, Vermont has turned in a decidedly progressive direction. (In contrast, New Hampshire remains a staunchly and safely Republican state). Michael Dukakis came very close to carrying Vermont, winning 48 percent of the vote there. Vermont's Governor from 1984–1990, Madeline Kunin, had a liberal record, particularly on education policy (attempting to equalize resources across the state). (She gave up her seat in 1990 and was replaced by a former governor, Republican Richard Snelling.) And the state's senior Senator, Democrat Patrick Leahy, had ADA ratings of 100 and 94 in 1989 and 1990. In the race for Vermont's at-large House seat in 1988, Bernard Sanders, the socialist former mayor of Burlington, Vermont's largest city, received 36 percent of the vote running as an independent. (The Democratic candidate received 19 percent, allowing the Republican to win with only 45 percent of the vote). Sanders built on that strong showing to win election to Congress as an Independent in 1990, becoming the first avowed socialist in Congress since the 1920s. Clearly, there is a large core of support for progressive policies in Vermont. Sanders's perceived successes in Burlington have left behind a strong progressive base. While he ran as a socialist opposed to the local Democratic Party, his local successes help point to the ways in which progressive Democrats can begin to build grass roots coalitions that can be expanded into broader areas.

Finally, Connecticut is the third New England state that George Bush carried which is clearly anything but a safe Republican state. As in Vermont, Bush's margin in Connecticut was substantially lower than his national victory, only 52 percent to 47 percent. Christopher Dodd, the state's senior Senator, is a liberal Democrat, receiving ADA ratings of 85 in 1988, 65 in 1989, and 61 in 1990. Dodd has been particularly active pushing a liberal, progressive agenda on foreign policy issues (he was one of the leading opponents of aid to the Nicaraguan Contras) and in the area of family policy (child care, parental leave). Dodd was easily reelected in 1986, winning 63 percent of the vote. Junior Senator Joseph Lieberman is, if anything, more liberal, especially on domestic issues, receiving ADA ratings of 75 and 83 in 1988 and 1990.

The Middle Atlantic states of New Jersey, Pennsylvania, Delaware, and Maryland also hold out hope for the Democrats. These states accounted for 54 electoral votes in 1988, but both New Jersey and Pennsylvania are proportionally shrinking and they will account for only 51 votes in 1992.

New Jersey was a fairly comfortable state for George Bush in 1988, as he won 56 percent of the vote. In fact, New Jersey is one of the states which has not voted for a Democratic presidential candidate since Lyndon Johnson. Still, both of New Jersey's Senators are liberal Democrats. Bill Bradley, the state's senior Senator, is often mentioned as a presidential candidate and had ADA ratings in 1989 and 1990 of 85 and 94. The state's junior Senator, Frank Lautenberg, is even more liberal, receiving ADA ratings of 80 and 100 in those two years. And while George Bush was carrying the state, Lautenberg was winning reelection against Republican Peter Dawkins with 54 percent of the vote. (Dawkins tried, in the campaign, to profit from painting Lautenberg as a "liberal.") And in 1989 (New Jersey is one of the two states in the country with odd-year gubernatorial elections), Democrat James Florio, another liberal Democrat (while in the House of Representatives in 1987 and 1988 he had ADA ratings of 92 and 80), was easily elected over conservative Republican Jim Courter. In his campaign Florio stressed his pro-choice position on the abortion issue.

Until 1991, Pennsylvania in some respects looked less promising than New Jersey. While both of New Jersey's Senators and its Governor are liberal Democrats, Pennsylvania had two Republican Senators. However, Dukakis came very close to carrying the state, losing only 51 percent to 48. (Jimmy Carter did carry the state in 1976.) Then, in 1991, the tragic death of Senator John Heinz in a airplane crash led to a series of events that vividly showed Pennsylvania's potential in a progressive coalition. Democratic Governor Robert Casey appointed a liberal Democrat, Harris Wofford, to fill the new vacancy until a special election could be held in November 1991. Attorney General Dick Thornburgh, a former Governor, resigned his post in the Bush Administration to run as the Republican candidate for Senator. It was, at the outset, expected to be an easy Republican victory. However, Wofford ran a spirited progressive campaign, hammering away at the failures of the Bush Administration in many areas of domestic policy, particularly health care, and was able to win a comfortable 55 percent victory.

By any measure, Pennsylvania is a highly competitive state. In recent years, the western half of the state (which has been heavily hit by the decline in the steel and coal industries) has been moving in a more Democratic direction, but the eastern half of the state has not. (In fact, Dukakis carried the western half of the state; Bush carried the eastern half.) Pennsylvania is not a state which either party will be able to take for granted, and it is also a state which, as Wofford has shown, an effective liberal, progressive Democrat can carry (especially if the Democrats can draw a large turnout among Philadelphia black voters to complement the party's seeming advantage in the western half of the state).

Delaware, the smallest of the Middle Atlantic states, is probably the least hospitable to progressive Democrats. The senior Senator, Joseph Biden, is a liberal Democrat. (He had an ADA rating of 90 in 1989; and 83 in 1990.) The sole Representative, Thomas Carper, is slightly more moderate (ADA ratings of 80 and 78 in 1989 and 1990 respectively.) The state last voted for a Democratic presidential candidate in 1976, and George Bush carried the state comfortably in 1988, with 56 percent of the vote. Still, the success of Biden and Carper indicates that progressive Democrats need not write off Delaware's 3 electoral votes (especially since much of the state is served by Philadelphia television, so that campaigning in eastern Pennsylvania will also bring publicity and attention in Delaware).

Maryland is the Middle Atlantic state which seems most hospitable to liberal Democrats. Michael Dukakis came very close to carrying the state, losing by only 51 percent to 48 percent, and the states two senators are both liberal Democrats. Paul Sarbanes received ADA ratings of 85 in 1989 and 83 in 1990, and easily won reelection in 1988 with 62 percent of the vote; Barbara Mikulski's ADA ratings in 1989 and 1990 were 90 and 94 (making the two, by ADA ratings, the third most liberal pair of Senators in the nation. The Senators of Massachusetts and New Jersey were more liberal). Additionally, the state's Governor, Democrat William Schaefer, has a reputation for using government as an active tool to solve state problems. He also took on the National Rifle Association and won, as Maryland voters passed a tough gun control referendum by a 58 to 42 margin in 1988.

The Midwest

The three large states in the industrial Midwest, Ohio, Illinois and Michigan, are also prime targets for progressive Democrats. All three suffered population losses in the 1980s, and each will lose 2 congressional seats (and electoral votes) after redistricting in 1990. While they accounted for 67 electoral votes in 1988, they will account for only 61 in 1992. Still, the same economic problems which led to the relative decline in the population of these three states leave them open to progressive Democratic appeals, particularly on economic issues. (Indiana, which is in the middle of these three states, is a safe Republican bastion in the region, even without a Republican Vice-Presidential candidate from the state on the ticket.)

Of these three states, Ohio went the most heavily for Bush in 1988, supporting him by a 55 to 44 margin. Still, liberal Democrats can, and do, win in Ohio. Both Senators John Glenn and Howard Metzenbaum are Democrats, as was former Governor Richard Celeste, who retired in 1990 and was replaced by Republican Anthony Voinovich. And while Glenn is often described as a moderate, not a liberal Democrat (in part because that is the way he tried to position himself in his unsuccessful 1984 presidential campaign), he did have ADA scores of 65 in 1989 and 89 in 1990. And Howard Metzenbaum clearly is, and has a reputation as, one of the most liberal members of the Senate. (His ADA scores in 1989 and 1990 were 95 and 78. It may also be the comparison with Metzenbaum that makes Glenn look like a "moderate.") Metzenbaum was up for reelection in 1988 and (like Frank Lautenberg of New Jersey) was targeted by Republicans as an incumbent they could beat because he was "too liberal." Still, Metzenbaum was easily reelected, with 57 percent of the vote.

Michigan also was carried fairly easily by George Bush with 54 percent. But, like Ohio, Michigan has two Democratic Senators and had a Democratic Governor, James Blanchard. And in all three cases, the liberal credentials are clear. Don Riegle had ADA ratings of 83 in 1990 and 85 in 1989 and easily won reelection with 60 percent of the vote at the same time Michael Dukakis was losing the state. The other Senator, Carl Levin, had ADA ratings of 80 and 78 in 1989 and 1990 and is the Senate's leading opponent of the death penalty (which does not seem to hurt him among working-class white Democratic voters in Michigan). Levin has also been an outspoken critic of the strategic defense initiative (Star Wars), pushing to reallocate that money to other causes. Governor Blanchard's policies of using state pension funds as venture capital to help stimulate manufacturing jobs and of providing more open access to college education for a time won him enormous popularity. Unfortunately, the fiscal problems of the state and a poor reelection campaign (which began with Blanchard forcing his Lieutenant-Governor off the ticket) led in 1990 to an upset victory by Republican John Engler. (The race was an extremely close one: Engler won by only 13,000 votes out of over 2 million cast.)

Finally, there is Illinois, like Pennsylvania, a highly competitive state in 1988 and likely to remain one in the foreseeable future. Bush narrowly carried the state in 1988, with 51 percent of the vote. Of the state's Senators, both Democrats, Alan Dixon is a moderate (ADA ratings of 55 in 1989 and 44 in 1990), but the other is liberal Paul Simon. Simon campaigned as a liberal in the 1988 presidential primaries and that campaigning did not seem to hurt his popularity in Illinois. (He had an ADA rating of 100 in 1989 and 94 in 1990.) Illinois has not voted for a Democratic presidential candidate since 1964, but it is a state which neither party can take for granted. Liberal Democrats stand a reasonable chance of winning, particularly if they can inspire a large turnout among Chicago's black population. (According to the 1990 census, 15 percent of Illinois' population was black, a higher percentage than Michigan (14), Ohio (11), or Pennsylvania (9)).

Three other states in the upper Midwest also hold out hope for the Democrats: North and South Dakota (with 6 electoral votes combined), and, more uncertainly, Missouri with 11 electoral votes. The other two midwestern states, Kansas and Nebraska, seem fairly safely in the Republican column. Kansas has not elected a Democratic Senator since 1932! And while Nebraska did elect Democrat Bob Kerrey to the Senate in 1988 with 57 percent of the vote, it does not seem like a rewarding territory for a liberal Democratic presidential candidate (unless, of course, that candidate is Senator Kerrey!). The Democrats might still learn something from Kerrey's opposition to the flag-burning laws—it helps that Kerrey is a decorated Vietnam Veteran—as that opposition has not hurt his popularity in conservative Nebraska. But the Dakotas, as we will see, offer real hope for Democratic votes. Kansas and Nebraska do not.

North and South Dakota, with 3 electoral votes apiece, have both shown a willingness to support progressive Democrats in statewide elections, particularly if they focus on populist economic themes. South Dakota's junior Senator, Thomas Daschle, by stressing themes of economic populism and redistribution, overcame attacks on his support for liberal policies (one ad attacked him for inviting Jane Fonda to testify before a congressional hearing) and defeated incumbent Republican James Abdnor in 1986. Since his election, Daschle has continued to push a liberal agenda as Co-chair of the Democrat's Senate Policy Committee. (His ADA ratings were 80 in 1981 and 83 in 1990.) South Dakota's sole Representative, Tim Johnson, is also a moderate-to-liberal Democrat (ADA scores of 85 and 67 in 1989 and 1990). And South Dakota was one of Michael Dukakis' stronger states, as he held George Bush to only 53 percent of the vote here.

North Dakota gave George Bush a comfortable 56 to 43 margin of victory. On the other hand, at the same time, North Dakota voters were reelecting Democratic Senator Quentin Burdick with 59 percent of the vote. Burdick (with ADA scores of 95 and 85 in 1987 and 1988, and 85 and 90 in 1989 and 1990) was attacked in the campaign as a "dangerous liberal," but that did not seem to upset the voters. In fact, their other Senator, Kent Conrad, and their Representative, Byron Dorgan, are also liberal Democrats. (Conrad's ADA scores in 1989 and 1990 were 70 and 67, Dorgan's were 85 and 72). Like the upper midwestern states of Iowa, Minnesota, and Wisconsin, the Dakotas are willing to vote for progressive, liberal Democrats, particularly those who stress issues of economic populism and redistribution.

Missouri, on the other hand, seems a more difficult state for liberal Democrats. Jimmy Carter carried the state in 1976, but the last time Missouri elected a liberal Democratic Senator was in 1980 when Thomas Eagleton won 52 percent of the vote. Missouri is competitive. George Bush won only 52 percent there in 1988, but the state usually elects Republicans to statewide office. Both Senators, Republicans John Danforth and Kit Bond, won narrow victories in the 1980s, though Danforth did win easy reelection in 1988 with 68 percent. The Democrats should not dismiss the state entirely. But election results in the 1980s do not hold as much hope in Missouri as in some of the other states we have examined. It seems that it would take an unusually large turnout in the black communities of St. Louis and Kansas City to push the state into the Democratic column.

California

Finally, there is one other state the Democrats need to look toward as they try to build an electoral majority: California. The nation's largest state, California had 47 electoral votes in 1988. That number will jump to 54 in 1992, giving California the highest percentage of total electoral votes in a single state (20 percent of the total needed for election) since the nineteenth century. Along with Hawaii, Washington, and Oregon, California forms the third geographical region where liberal Democrats can expect to be competitive. (The other Pacific Rim state, Alaska, is safely Republican. Both of its Senators are conservative Republicans, and Michael Dukakis received only 36 percent of the vote in the state in 1988.) George Bush narrowly carried California with 51 percent in 1988. California's senior Senator, Alan Cranston, is a liberal Democrat (ADA scores of 85 and 100 in 1989 and 1990), who narrowly won election to a fourth term in 1986 with 50 percent of the vote. Statewide races in California are usually close. Republican Senator Pete Wilson has won election twice with under 53 percent, and Republican Governor George Dukemejian was initially elected in an extremely close contest with Los Angeles Mayor Tom Bradley, winning with 49 percent of the vote. Similarly, in the 1990 gubernatorial election, Republican Senator Pete Wilson won a narrow victory over Democrat Diane Feinstein (49 percent to 46). In addition, the fastest growing parts of California's rapidly growing population are its minority communities. According to 1990 census figures, 26 percent of the population here was of Hispanic origin, 7 percent was black, and 10 percent was Asian. These percentages have surely increased since then, and liberal Democrats can, clearly, compete in California. Given its size, both parties are sure to target a vast proportion of their resources to California throughout the 1990s, and there is no reason to believe that California will be anything but a highly competitive state, with both parties having a good chance of winning its enormous electoral prize.

The states discussed in this chapter so far will have a total of 305 electoral votes in 1992 (see Table 5-2), 35 more than is needed to win the Presidency. (If you ignore Missouri and Delaware, which seem competitive but more safely Republican than

Table 5-2

Building a Progressive Electoral College Majority

The Core: States Carried by Michael Dukakis in 1988

State	Electoral Votes		State	Electoral Votes	
	1988	1992		1988	1992
Massachusetts	13	12	Washington	10	11
Rhode Island	4	4	Oregon	7	7
New York	36	33	Hawaii	4	4
Wisconsin	11	11	West Virginia	6	5
Minnesota	10	10	Dist. of Columbia	3	3
Iowa	8	7	Total	112	107

States with Strong Progressive Bases

State			State		
Vermont	3	3	Ohio	23	21
Maine	4	4	Illinois	24	22
Connecticut	8	8	Michigan	20	18
New Jersey	16	15	North Dakota	3	3
Pennsylvania	25	23	South Dakota	3	3
Maryland	10	10	Missouri	11	11
Delaware	3	3	California	47	54
			TOTAL	200	198

Other Possibilities

State			State		
Montana	4	3	Georgia	12	13
Colorado	8	8	Arkansas	6	6
New Mexico	5	5	Tennessee	11	11
			TOTAL	46	46

States Where High Minority Turnout Is Needed

State			State		
Texas	29	32	Mississippi	7	7
Louisiana	10	9	North Carolina	13	14
			TOTAL	59	62

the other states, there are still 291 electoral votes.) This does not leave much room for error. The loss of California, obviously, would be devastating. And in the long run, progressive Democrats clearly need to build a broader national coalition. The point here, however, is that winning the Presidency does not have to wait until that coalition is built and broadened. Progressive Democrats can pursue the Presidency at the same time as they attempt to rebuild local progressive coalitions. And, in fact, such a presidential candidacy (and victory) would be a major impetus to efforts to build such coalitions. There clearly is a solid core of states that have shown a willingness to elect liberal Democrats. And these states can form a core constituency on which the Democrats can build a national majority. (As we shall see, there are other states the Democrats might also look to for electoral votes.) One problem for the Democrats, however, is that within this core states differ in terms of the kinds of progressive issues which seem to have the most appeal. In particular, the midwestern states seem most attracted to issues of economic redistribution, while the Pacific Rim states seem most attracted to issues of cultural, lifestyle liberalism. (The northeastern states seem to fall in-between). Michael Barone and Grant Ujifusa write in *The Almanac of American Politics*:

> The liberalism that appeals to California is cultural, not economic. The redistributionist policies that may appeal to farmers in Iowa or blacks in Michigan and the trade policies that are thought to appeal to factory workers in Pennsylvania and Ohio are probably vote-losers in California. . . . Those who look hopefully and with some reason to California as a building block for a new liberal majority must reckon with the differences between its liberalism and that of other states essential to their strategy.[7]

But such sentiments overlook a large number of policies which can bind these two types of liberalism together. I will detail these policies in the final part of the book, but for now we need to note two things. First, there clearly are areas of overlap in support. Issues of economic planning (including zoning laws and low-income housing needs), rebuilding the infrastructure (which by increasing investment in mass transit will appeal to low-growth, California social liberals and creates jobs for working-class economic liberals), educational reform, and protecting the environment can cut across these supposed divisions. And second, as noted above, the fastest growing part of the California population is its poor, minority population. Much of this population has been left behind in the rapid expansion of the California economy.

And consequently, there is greater potential for building support in California on issues of economic populism than may seem evident at first glance.

Building a Democratic Majority III: Other Possible Sources of Support

The states discussed above can add up to more than the 270 electoral votes needed for a presidential election victory. But they are not the only states that the Democrats have a chance of carrying with a liberal candidate. There are a few other states in the South and the Mountain West, the two parts of the country completely left out of the discussion so far, which also show a willingness to elect liberal Democrats to statewide office.

The Mountain West

In many ways, the Mountain West is the most Republican part of the country. Wyoming, Arizona (which last voted for a Democratic presidential candidate in 1948, the longest Republican streak in the country), Utah, Nevada, and Idaho all supported George Bush by overwhelming margins (from a low for Bush of 59 percent in Nevada to a high of 66 percent in Utah). In addition, none of these states has shown any propensity to elect liberal Democrats to statewide office. They have elected a few moderate Democrats, such as Senator Dennis DeConcini of Arizona (ADA ratings of 60 in 1989 and 61 in 1990), Harry Reid of Nevada (ADA ratings of 65 in 1989 and 61 in 1990), and Governor Cecil Andrus of Idaho. Andrus was elected in spite of his opposition to the National Rifle Association, whom he often calls the "gun nuts of the world." (Andrus attacked the NRA for opposing a ban on armor piercing bullets by noting that he had never seen an animal wearing a bullet-proof vest.) But these five states seem likely to provide a safe Republican base of 24 electoral votes (an increase of one, in Arizona, from 1988).

The other three states of the Mountain West, Montana, Colorado and New Mexico, however, do offer hope to liberal Democrats. All three of these states were competitive in 1988. George Bush won only 53 percent of the vote in Colorado and 52 percent in New Mexico and Montana. In some ways, Montana's politics is a cross between the Dakotas to its east and the Mountain States of Idaho and Wyoming to its south. It has one liberal Democratic Senator, Max Baucus (ADA scores of 80 in 1989 and 56 in 1990). The state's economy is not particularly strong, and the need to open up foreign markets to the vast timber and mineral resources of Montana makes economic populist appeals more resonant here than in some of the other Rocky Mountain states. Montana had 4 electoral votes in 1988, but that will decline to 3 in 1992.

Colorado, the largest of the Rocky Mountain states with 8 electoral votes, has also shown a willingness to elect liberal Democrats. Gary Hart, of course, was twice elected to the Senate there, and one of its current Senators, Timothy Wirth, has also had success pushing for progressive, liberal policies. (Wirth's ADA ratings in 1989 and 1990 were 95 and 83, respectively). Wirth has been a leader in the fight to create a policy to deal with global warming, among other issues. In addition, the Denver area has a rapidly growing Hispanic population. Hispanics accounted for 13 percent of the population in Colorado in 1990, and that number has grown since then.

The large Hispanic population of New Mexico also helps make the state a competitive one for liberal Democrats. 1990 census figures indicated that 38 percent of New Mexico's population was Hispanic. And that growing part of the population provides a strong Democratic base in this usually Republican part of the nation. The state's Democratic Senator, Jeff Bingaman, has a moderate-to-liberal voting record (ADA scores of 65 and 67 in 1989 and 1990) and easily withstood a challenge in 1988, when his opponent focused on attacking him as a liberal. (Bingaman won with 63 percent of the vote). New Mexico's 5 electoral votes are not ones which the Republicans can take for granted, particularly if turnout is high in the Hispanic (and Native American) sections of the state.

The South

The South is the other part of the country where the Democrats have not done well in recent presidential elections. Much of the South did support Jimmy Carter in 1976, but only Georgia did so in 1980, and the entire region voted relatively heavily for George Bush in 1988. Still, not all of the South is hopeless. In particular, three states seem to offer some chance for liberal Democrats: Georgia, Arkansas, and Tennessee. Georgia did give George Bush 60 percent of the vote in 1988. However, the state's junior Senator, Wyche Fowler, is clearly a liberal Democrat. His ADA ratings in 1989 and 1990 were 60 and 72, respectively. And Fowler built his electoral coalition around Georgia's large black population, 27 percent of the total in 1990 (Fowler represented a congressional district with a black majority for ten years before running for the Senate), and liberal whites. In addition, Atlanta and its economy provide a different flavor to Georgia politics from what one finds in other southern states. This is not to say that Georgia is radically different from the rest of the South. It is not. But it is different enough that a reasonable turnout among the black population can make a liberal Democrat competitive there.

Arkansas, which gave George Bush 56 percent of its vote in 1988, has shown an even greater propensity to vote for liberal Democrats for statewide office. Both of its Senators, Dale Bumpers and David Pryor, and its Governor, Bill Clinton, fit this description. (Bumpers and Pryor, respectively, had ADA ratings of 90 and 80 in 1989 and 72 and 67 in 1990). Arkansas is a relatively poor state with fewer resources than most of its southern neighbors, which makes economic liberalism attractive there. And like most southern states, it has a fairly large black population (16 percent in 1990).

Finally, there is Tennessee, which has 11 electoral votes. George Bush won a comfortable 58 percent of the vote in 1988. But Tennessee, like Arkansas, has managed to elect two liberal Democratic Senators. James Sasser, who had ADA scores of 85 and 72 in 1989 and 1990, was reelected in 1988 with 65 percent of the vote. Tennessee's junior Senator, Al Gore, ran in the 1988 presidential election as a southern "moderate" alternative to the other Democratic candidates. But except for foreign policy issues, where Gore is more conservative than many Democrats, Gore's record is clearly liberal. His ADA ratings of 55 in 1989 and 78 in 1990 reflect that division in his record. In fact, Gore's domestic policy positions were probably closer to traditional liberal Democratic activist government policies than were those of nominee Michael Dukakis. Gore came across as a "conservative alternative" because of his foreign policy positions, including support for the reflagging operation in the Persian Gulf and for humanitarian aid to the Nicaragua Contras (he did oppose military aid). He also was one of only a handful of Democratic Senators to support the authorization of the use of force in the Persian Gulf. Tennessee will support liberal Democrats.

The largest state in the South, Texas, will jump from 29 to 32 electoral votes in 1992. Texas has not been particularly hospitable to liberal Democrats. Michael Dukakis received only 43 percent of the vote there in 1988, even with moderate Texas Democrat Lloyd Bentsen as his running mate. Still, there are some signs of hope in Texas (certainly much more hope than in the South's other large prize, Florida). First, Texans have elected a few liberal Democrats to statewide office: most prominently, the current governor, Ann Richards, who defeated conservative Republican Clayton Williams in a very close race (51 percent to 49) in spite of being outspent 2 to 1; Attorney General Jim Mattox; and former Agricultural Commissioner Jim Hightower (who, however, was defeated in 1990 in a bid for a third term). Hightower, in particular, has had success by running on a platform that stressed issues of economic populism. Second, in 1982 Democrat Mark White was able to win the Governor's race based on the success of a massive voter registration and get-out-the-vote drive. Third, the state has a large base of poor black and Hispanic voters. In 1990, census figures indicated that 26 percent of the population was Hispanic and 12 percent was black. There is, therefore, a large base for the Democrats to draw on.

A large black population also holds out some hope in other southern states. Louisiana was the southern state where Dukakis received his highest proportion of the vote (44 percent). And one of its Senators, John Breaux, while clearly a moderate, not a liberal Democrat (ADA scores of 40 and 33 in 1989 and 1990), did rely on a populist appeal and a large black turnout to win election in 1986. Louisiana's large black population (31 percent of the state in 1990, second in terms of percentage to Mississippi) and poor economy make it a target for progressive policies. The 1991 gubernatorial election in which Democrat Edwin Edwards defeated David Duke shows the potential impact of a large minority turnout. While most analyses have stressed Louisiana voter's acceptance of Duke's very conservative appeal (and racist background) and the fact that Duke won 55 percent of the white vote in that election, what is also important is that the high turnout among minority voters, who were almost unanimously supportive of Edwards, led to an easy victory for the former Governor. Obviously, Edwards is not a progressive Democrat. But the large proportion of minority voters in Louisiana does provide a core on which a progressive coalition can build. Winning the "white vote" is not necessary.

Similarly, Mississippi, with the largest percentage of black voters in the country (36 percent of the population in 1990) and a very poor economy, has the potential to support progressive Democrats. Wayne Dowdy tried running a populist economic campaign against Republican Trent Lott in the 1986 senatorial election and won 46 percent of the vote. Increasing the percentage of black voters who go to the polls in Mississippi could change the nature of politics in a state which gave 60 percent of its vote to George Bush in 1988.

North Carolina, the home state of archconservative Senator Jesse Helms, is also not as clearly Republican as one might think. Helms has never had an easy election victory, winning only 52 percent of the vote in 1984 and by the same proportion in 1990 against Harvey Gantt. Gantt, the former Mayor of Charlotte, is an African-American, and ran his campaign as an unrepentant liberal. His surprisingly strong showing (in spite of an enormous financial disadvantage) points to the potential long-term viability of a progressive strategy even in the South (especially if turnout among minority citizens can be increased). And the state's other Senator, Terry Sanford, is a moderate-liberal Democrat, receiving ADA ratings of 65 in 1989 and 67 in 1990. In addition, there is a core liberal Democratic constituency in the black community (22 percent of the population in 1990) and in the Raleigh-Durham-Chapel Hill Research Triangle (home of North Carolina State, Duke University and the University of North Carolina). As in Mississippi, raising turnout among black voters seems to be the key to building a progressive Democratic Party in North Carolina.

Three other states with large black populations, Alabama, South Carolina, and Virginia, seem to offer less hope for progressive Democrats. Still, with black voters making up 25 percent of Alabama's population in 1990, and 30 percent of South Carolina's, there is a core to build on in the future. And Virginia, with a 19 percent black population, in 1990 elected Douglas Wilder as the first black Governor in the United States since reconstruction. But, with the exception of the abortion issue, Wilder downplayed liberal policies and stressed his moderation on the issues, calling for a "defense of the free enterprise system" and "holding the line on taxes." His election does show the potential of the abortion issue to drive wedges into the Republican Party, but his stress on not being a "liberal" makes his victory less of a model for progressive Democrats in the South than is sometimes argued.

Finally, there are two states in the South, Kentucky and Florida, plus Oklahoma, which seem to offer no hope for progressive Democrats. Florida, the South's second largest state, growing from 21 to 25 electoral votes in 1992, looks safely in the Republican column. The percentage of the population which is black is only (by southern standards, only), 14 percent. And while the Hispanic population is 12 percent of the population, much of it is made up of Cuban-Americans who are much more Republican than the Puerto-Rican Americans who dominate in northeastern Hispanic communities or the Mexican-Americans who are prevalent in Texas, California, and the rest of the West. George Bush received 61 percent of the Florida vote in 1988. Lawton Chiles in 1990 did manage to defeat Republican incumbent Governor Bob Martinez by stressing the need to rebuild decaying social relations, his unwillingness to accept contributions of greater than $100, and a pro-choice abortion position. His campaign illustrates the potential in running against "big money" (I will return to this theme in Chapter 9) and the popularity of pro-choice abortion positions, but it is still hard to imagine Florida voting for a progressive Democratic presidential candidate in the foreseeable future.

Similarly, Kentucky seems safely Republican. It does have a moderate Democratic Senator, Wendell Ford (ADA scores of 45 in 1989 and 39 in 1990), but it is hard to envision progressive or liberal Democratic victories in Kentucky. And Oklahoma may be the safest state for the Republicans outside of the Mountain West. It does have one Democratic Senator, David Boren, but he is one of the most conservative Democrats in the Senate (ADA ratings of 30 in 1989 and 56 in 1990). George Bush won a healthy 58 percent of the vote there in 1988, and in spite of some economic difficulties in the 1980s, Oklahoma seems safely Republican.

Conclusion: An Electoral Strategy

Nevertheless, as we have seen, there are other states beyond the core where progressive Democrats can hope to be competitive. The three Mountain West States and Georgia, Arkansas, and Tennessee have a total of 46 electoral votes, and Texas brings an additional 32. Additionally, high black voter turnout could lead to the capture of Louisiana, Mississippi, and/or North Carolina with as many as another 30 electoral votes. When you add all of these to the 305 votes in the core, you get a total of 413 electoral votes. And that leaves a lot of room for error. If a progressive Democrat can pick up only a few of these states, then even losing two of the large midwestern industrial states would not be fatal, though losing California still seems likely to be an insurmountable problem at this time.

On the other hand, a strategy designed to appeal to southern moderates is almost bound to fail. First of all, such an appeal will weaken the party in its core constituency. Trying to win the votes of conservative white Democrats in the South will not help the party in Pennsylvania, California, Illinois, or Michigan. The kinds of issues which can mobilize Democratic constituencies in the core—issues of economic populism, the environment, fairness in tax policy, slowing down defense spending to increase social services, and the like—will appeal to southern blacks and poor southern whites. But such a strategy will not "recapture the white South." Rather, those are precisely the kinds of issues which have driven much of the white South into the Republican Party in recent presidential elections. Recapturing the "white South" seems to require a strategy which alienates the Democratic core. And abandoning the Democrats' core constituency to win these southern voters back seems fruitless.

Second, the long-term future of the Democratic Party depends on bringing black and Hispanic voters into the electorate. In the long run, such action will strengthen the progressive wing of the Democratic Party and help rebuild a majority coalition. This is important not only in the urban areas of the Northeast, Midwest, and California (New York, Philadelphia, Chicago, Detroit, Los Angeles), but also in Texas and much of the South. And appeals to conservative southern whites will only undercut this effort. It makes more sense, it seems to me, for the Democrats to build for the future by reinvigorating the party at the grass roots level and bringing blacks, Hispanics and poor whites back to politics. In the long run, that will, once again, make the Democrats competitive in the South. And in the short run it will still allow the Democrats to compete nationally. The Democrats need to reconnect the public with their government. Voter apathy and alienation, especially among minorities and the poor, has been driving the nation in a conservative direction. Bringing these voters back into politics, even at the expense of more conservative or moderate southern white voters, can only help the party in the long run.

There is, clearly, then, a geographic constituency on which to build a progressive Democratic Party. Such a strategy involves giving up, certainly in the short run, on all, or most, of the Mountain West and the South, at least as part of a presidential electoral majority coalition. (Obviously, there are local areas within these regions which will support progressive politics, and the Democrats should continue to build such local support, even if their presidential strategy does not target these states). But there still are more than enough states which have a history of supporting progressive Democrats in statewide elections to indicate that a progressive Democratic presidential candidate can win the Presidency. As I hope to show in the final part of the book, the Democrats need to stress rebuilding the party at the local level. But such a strategy should not ignore presidential politics. Who is at the top of the ticket has enormous implications for what happens lower down in the party. National policies can be used to reinvigorate local politics. And consequently, progressive Democrats need to have a reasonable strategy for winning the Presidency as well.

Winning the Presidency, then, requires a strategy that focuses on the Northeast, Midwest, and West Coast. A few other states may also offer support, but the primary focus should be in those areas. There are the states with a history of support for liberal policies; taken together, the states in these regions will have 305 electoral votes in 1992. But creating a coherent platform which can appeal to the broad interests present in this potential coalition will not be easy. The liberalism of California, for example, seems very different in many ways from the economic populism which dominates the liberalism of the Midwest. Before turning, therefore, to a more detailed look at a winning progressive strategy, we need to take a closer look at the Democratic and Republican coalitions and the sources of cohesion and conflict within the two parties. In the next two chapters, we will explore these questions carefully, breaking down the parties, not in a geographical sense as we have done here, but in terms of the demographic groups which make up each of the party coalitions.

6

The Democrats: Whatever Happened to the New Deal Coalition?

In 1932, Franklin Roosevelt began fashioning the coalition that was to dominate American politics for at least the next thirty years. The New Deal coalition of the Democratic Party dominated American politics through the 1960s. Since then, the Democrats have seen their dominance fade, but the New Deal coalition is not as dead as some would have it, and it still presents the foundation for a future Democratic majority coalition. The New Deal coalition was made up of five basic groups: white southerners, Catholics, union members, Jews, and blacks. The primary glue which held the coalition together was (outside of the South) support for the use of active government to help lower- and middle-class Americans. As we shall see, while there has been some slippage, these groups, with the exception of white southerners, still are relatively loyal to the Democratic Party. In this chapter we will look at what has happened to the New Deal coalition and the forces which can help to revitalize it, not in exactly the same form it took in the heyday of the New Deal, but in accord with the forces which drive American politics in the 1990s.

The Transformation of the New Deal Coalition

There is only one group which has deserted the New Deal coalition almost entirely, and that is southern whites.[1] In the period from 1952 through 1960, white southerners gave the Democratic Party an average 48 point advantage in party identification. (That is, the percentage of Democrats minus the percentage of Republicans was 48).[2] By 1986, the same group gave the Republican Party an 18 percent advantage. The loss of the white southern vote is clear and unmistakable. As we saw in the last chapter, much of the South is safely Republican in presidential voting. Even Jimmy Carter failed to carry a majority of white southerners. He was able to win the South on the basis of an overwhelming level of support from southern blacks. And it was the issue of race that drove white southerners from the Democratic Party.[3] The battles within the Democratic Party over issues of civil rights and activist government pitted southern Democrats against the rest of the party from 1948 (when southern Democrats deserted the party to support then Democratic Senator Strom Thurmond and the "Dixiecrat" ticket) right on through 1968, when they rallied behind the candidacy of George Wallace.

But in many ways, southern whites were an anomalous part of the New Deal coalition to begin with. Most of the coalition was attracted to the Democratic Party for economic reasons. Relatively affluent southern whites were always out of place. And trying to keep them satisfied always had the tendency of pushing the Democrats in a conservative direction. Democrats, such as Charles Robb of Virginia and Sam Nunn of Georgia, who focus on rewinning the South as the way for the Democrats to regain power, continue in that tradition. But such policies only serve to weaken the glue which tends to hold the rest of the party together. The Democrats can target poor and middle-class southern whites with the same kinds of economic appeals which will bring the party together (though the conservatism of these groups on race issues can still be an obstacle). I will turn to these appeals in Chapter Eight. However, not only are the Democrats unlikely to win an election by bringing affluent white southerners back into the fold, they are also likely to weaken their appeal to their core constituency with such an approach. If the New Deal coalition requires the return of white southerners, then the Democrats should declare the New Deal coalition dead.

If racial issues helped drive southern whites from the Democratic coalition, they helped solidify the party's hold on black voters. Blacks are, clearly, the most loyal Democratic group in the country. Ninety percent of the blacks who voted in 1988 supported Michael Dukakis, and there is little indication that this loyalty is fading.[4] Since 1964, when Lyndon Johnson made clear that the Democrats had at the national level abandoned their southern white supporters on the issue of civil rights, and the Republicans nominated a candidate, Barry Goldwater, who opposed civil rights legislation, the Democrats have been much more progressive on issues of civil rights for minorities than the Republicans. And since Richard Nixon ran for the Presidency in 1968, the Republicans have pursued a "southern strategy" designed to win over disaffected southern whites to the Republican Party. This has worked. But it has also helped to solidify black support for the Democratic Party. Ronald Reagan was reluctant to support the establishment of the Martin Luther King national holiday, and the only real opposition to that proposal came from Republicans. Similarly, Reagan's nomination of Judge Robert Bork to the Supreme Court seemed to threaten many of the civil rights gains of the last two decades and led to strong opposition from civil rights groups. Blacks remain a key element in the Democratic coalition, and their proportion in the population continues to grow.

Similarly, Jewish voters remain relatively loyal to the Democrats. In spite of increasing affluence and economic success, 73 percent of Jewish voters supported Michael Dukakis. And, in fact, blacks and Jews were the only two major demographic groups in the nation to register decreased support for Ronald Reagan between 1980 and 1984. In part, this continuing support for Democrats reflects the fact that Jewish voters tend to take liberal positions on many national political issues in spite of their continuing economic success. But part of it also reflects the strength of the evangelical Christian Right within the Republican Party. As long as that association remains strong, and it is likely to remain strong, it will not be easy for Republicans to win lasting support among Jewish voters.

Union members, too, remain loyal to the Democratic Party, although there has been a good deal of slippage here. Petrocik and Steeper note that while union members gave the Democrats an average 30 percent partisan advantage through the 1970s, that advantage had shrunk to about 10 percent by the 1980s, and union members supported Dukakis only by a very thin 53 to 46 margin.[5] Part of this slippage reflects the economic success of unions. Many more union households are middle class, and, consequently, more attracted to Republican economic policies. This is particularly so in the area of taxation, where Democrats are seen as the party likely to raise taxes. But it also reflects more conservative views on social policy and the view, noted in Chapter Two, that Democrats are too supportive of civil rights and minorities. Also, it should be noted that the percentage of workers belonging to unions has continued to decline. Thus, even if union members continue to be supportive of the Democratic Party, they count for less than they did in the past.

Finally, Catholics too have slipped in their support for the Democratic Party. In fact, by 1986 Catholics gave no partisan advantage to either party. They were equally likely to be Democrats as Republicans, a substantial decline from the 1960s when Catholics gave the Democrats a 30 percent partisan advantage. And the Catholic vote in 1988 was almost a dead heat, with Dukakis winning 51 percent to Bush's 48 percent.[6] Still, Catholic loyalty to the Democrats has not disappeared. As E. J. Dionne notes, while the weakening of Catholic loyalty to the Democratic Party is clear, they "have hardly embraced the Republicans with enthusiasm."[7] And as Henry Kenski notes, "a plurality of Catholics remain Democratic and the Catholic voter is more likely to identify as a Democrat or Independent rather than as a Republican."[8] Increasing affluence has pushed Catholic voters away from the Democratic Party, but not as much as might be expected, since Catholics still tend to be more liberal on a variety of economic and social issues than white Protestants. This liberalism is not as distinctive as the liberalism of Jewish voters, but it still tends to push Catholics in a Democratic direction. (We will return to these issues shortly.)

Thus, while weakened, with the exception of white southerners, the core of the New Deal coalition still favors the Democratic Party. In addition, there are other groups which in recent years have become more favorable toward the Democratic Party.

Women and Hispanics: New Groups in the Democratic Coalition

One of the most remarked-on political phenomena in the 1980s was the emergence of the gender gap.[9] Women are more supportive than men of Democratic candidates and the Democratic Party. The size of the gap in the 1988 election depends upon which survey one looks at. As reported by Abramson, Aldrich, and Rohde, the National Election Study found Bush and Dukakis each won 50 percent of the women's vote, whereas Bush won the male vote 56 to 43. The ABC News/*Washington Post* poll showed Dukakis winning 53 percent of the women's vote but only 44 percent of the male vote, while the Gallup poll found Dukakis losing the women's vote 48 to 52 for Bush (in the Gallup poll, Dukakis's standing among men was even worse). Abramson, Aldrich, and Rohde conclude,

> If the vote had been restricted to women, the election result would have been very close, and . . . Dukakis might have emerged with a slight majority of the popular vote. But even though there were more female voters than male voters, Bush's sizable lead among men led to a clear majority in the popular vote.[10]

Similarly, it is clear that women are more likely than men to identify themselves as Democrats. In June 1988, for example, Gallup found that 45 percent of women identified themselves as

Democrats compared to only 40 percent of men.[11]

The causes for the gender gap are also a matter of dispute, but the evidence seems to suggest that the gap is mostly a phenomena among women of higher socioeconomic status, reflecting their general social liberalism when compared with upper-income men. For example, the 1988 ABC News Election Day poll found that among high-status women, party identification was 40 percent Democratic and 38 percent Republican. Among high-status men, the figures were 28 Democratic and 48 Republican. (Among lower-status men and women, the Democrats are the party of choice.) Similarly, high-status women had ideological self-identifications of 35 percent liberal and 40 percent conservative, compared with figures of 23 percent liberal and 58 percent conservative for high-status men. ("High status" was defined in this survey as being a college graduate with family income of $50,000 or more.)[12]

This liberalism is seen not so much in the distribution of opinion on issues such as abortion or women's rights (men and women are equally supportive of women's rights, and attitudes on abortion show little gender differences), but in the salience of such issues. That is, women are more likely to find such issues to be important factors when they think about politics.[13] Women also tend to be more liberal on foreign policy issues and in areas of economic spending priorities.[14] Since women do make up a majority of the electorate, they are another potential building block for a new liberal Democratic coalition. It is important, I think, not to overemphasize the gender gap. As Herbert Weisberg noted in examining the 1984 election, "the largest voting differences [are] on the basis of race and income, followed by differences based on marital status, religion, gender and region."[15] Income, race, and religion are all more distinguishing characteristics than gender when partisan differences are being examined. Still, given the enormous size of women as a group, the Democrats should certainly not overlook the gap, especially since it reflects a greater commitment to progressive policies on the part of women.

The other group which the Democrats can use to rebuild their coalition is Hispanic voters. Hispanics are one of the fastest-growing segments of the population as a result of both immigration and high birth rates. And Hispanics tend to be very Democratic. In 1988, Hispanics supported Dukakis by a 64 percent-to-36 percent margin according to the National Election Study and a 69-to-31 margin according to the NBC News/*Wall Street Journal* poll. This was a margin surpassed only among blacks and Jews. And a 1988 Gallup poll found party identification among Hispanics to favor the Democrats over the Republicans by 51 to 23. Note that these differences mask differences within the Hispanic community. In particular, Cuban-Americans, who are heavily concentrated in South Florida, are much more conservative and Republican than Mexican-American or Puerto Rican-Americans. Thus, in Florida Hispanic voters supported George Bush by a 68-to-32 margin, whereas in Texas Hispanic voters supported Michael Dukakis by a 79-to-21 margin.[16] (That is one reason why Florida is so safely Republican at the presidential level.) When you get away from Florida, the potential for Hispanic voters to help build a Democratic majority is great. Such voters are attracted to progressive economic policies and strong support for civil rights, although they often are somewhat more conservative on issues of social policy.

Thus, there are six major groups the Democrats need to build on: blacks, Jews, Hispanics, women, Catholics and union members. What we need to turn to now is the forces that tend to pull these groups together and the forces that tend to push them apart.

Sources of Cohesion

Economic issues are clearly the glue which binds the Democratic coalition together. In fact, in some ways income differences are more important than the differences between the groups discussed above. The poorer an individual is, the more likely he or she is to support the Democratic Party. The richer an individual is, the more likely he or she is to support the Republicans. Table

Table 6-1

Partisanship and 1988 Vote by Income (in percent)

Household Income	Identify as Democrat	Identify as Republican	Identify as Independent
$40,000 and over	34	37	29
$25,000–$39,999	41	30	29
$15,000–$24,999	43	28	29
Under $15,000	51	22	27

	Voted for Dukakis	Voted for Bush
$40,000 and over	37	62
$30,000–39,999	39	60
$20,000–$29,999	47	51
$10,000–$19,999	53	45
Under $10,000	64	33

Data for party identification and income are from *The Gallup Report*, September 1988, p. 6. Data for vote and income are from the *New York Times*/CBS News poll, *New York Times*, November 10, 1988, p. B6.

6-1 documents the income gap in party identification and in the 1988 presidential vote. As can be seen, the less well-off people are, the more Democratic they become as voters. And this trend has been increasing. As Thomas Edsall has documented, the Democratic Party has gained strength among those in the bottom third of the electorate, so much so that economic differences are now a much stronger factor in partisanship than at any time in the recent past.[17] And as Kevin Phillips, the conservative Republican political analyst, has noted, the growing gap between rich and poor in the United States creates strong potential for building a social/political movement based on the politics of class.[18]

The data in Table 6-2 show the striking differences between the top and bottom third of the electorate in income terms in the 1980s as opposed to the 1950s and 1960s. Whereas there was a 13 percent difference in the partisan leanings of the lower and upper third of the electorate in the 1950s (with all three groups favoring the Democrats!), by the 1980s there were 30-to-40 per-

Table 6-2

Parisanship of Income Groups, 1952–1986

Income	1952–1960	1964–1968	1972–1976	1980	1984	1986
Lower	16	25	20	25	12	6
Middle	17	23	16	8	0	−14
Upper	3	5	−6	−15	−20	−25

Numbers are derived by subtracting the Republican percentage from the Democratic percentage. Among the lower third of the population in income betwen 1952 and 1960, for example, Democrats had a 16 percentage point edge.

Source: John Petrocik and Frederick Steeper, "The Political Landscape in 1988," *Public Opinion*, September/October 1987, p. 42.

cent differences, with the lower third of the electorate leaning toward the Democrats and the upper third favoring the Republicans. Commenting on this trend, Petrocik and Steeper wrote:

> What is striking today is [the] magnitude and the preeminence of income among the various measures of socioeconomic status. While income, education, and occupation used to be roughly comparable measures of social status, that is no longer the case. Family income now stands out for the strength and consistency of its relationship to partisanship.[19]

Similarly, the widespread appeal to the Democratic coalition of issues of economic redistribution and justice to the Democratic coalition is clear. For example, in 1989 Gallup found that 64 percent of those with family incomes under $20,000 supported an increase in spending for job training programs, while 24 percent supported no change in current levels, and only 8 percent desired less spending. And among self-identified Democrats, 61 percent supported increases in job training. Similarly, 85 percent of self-identified Democrats in a 1988 Gallup survey supported increasing the minimum wage from $3.35 to $5.05, as did 82 percent of Catholics and 89 percent of African-Americans.[20]

Economic appeals and issues, then, are the glue which holds the Democratic Party together. While there are some groups (such as upper-status women and upper-status Jews) who do not fit this economic division, most of the groups which support the Democratic coalition are concentrated in the lower half of the economic structure. It is important, then, for the Democrats to raise issues of economic justice and fairness (not only for the poor but also for the middle class). In fact, such issues are also useful in attracting support from all parts of the Democratic coalition, not just the poorer ones. Catholics, women, and Jews are all groups which are strongly supportive of policies of redistribution even when income is taken into account. Kenski, Greeley, and Wald note greater willingness to spend money to help the poor among Catholics than among economically comparable Protestants,[21] and greater support among women for such policies is also well documented.[22] Focusing on such issues can only help bind the Democratic Party together.[23]

There are, however, other issues which also tend to bind the Democrats together. Improving education and cleaning up the environment are two areas where the Democrats can find common ground. As we have seen, there is a strong national consensus in favor of public activity in both of these areas. The Democrats should not hesitate to push for such action. For example, according to a July 1988 Gallup survey, 71 percent of Democrats felt we should spend more money on education. And all major Democratic groups exhibited such support: 67 percent of women, 86 percent of blacks, 72 percent of union members, 67 percent of Catholics, and 67 percent of those with family incomes under $30,000 wanted more spent on education. Similarly, according to a 1990 Gallup survey, 73 percent of Democrats felt the public was not concerned enough about environmental problems. And this sentiment was shared by 74 percent of those with family incomes under $20,000, 69 percent of Catholics, and 67 percent of blacks.[24]

It is true that environmental controls can, in the short run, cause economic dislocation, and thus it is sometimes argued that such issues will separate socially liberal upper-status citizens from economically liberal lower-status citizens. While this tension does at times emerge (as in the battle between environmentalists and the logging industry and loggers over owls in the Pacific Northwest), there is more common ground available than tension. It is crucial that the Democrats couple environmental action with protection for displaced workers (such as job training or retraining, extended unemployment, and the like). Such a coupling under a rubric of fairness is unlikely to meet stiff opposition from the public. In fact, public support is likely to be quite high. The public does not object to "welfare" programs which are seen as legitimate, and supporting displaced workers is something the public does in fact support.

Environmental protection with clear social choices about the costs of growth and development is, then, a policy arena which can bind social liberals concerned about the environment with lower-class Democrats concerned with protecting jobs and opportunities. The "California-Midwest" coalition which often seems so hard to fashion could find common ground here. In fact, as we shall see in Chapter 7, it is the Republican Party which is likely to face strong divisions over such issues. Only a focus on a trade-off that does not have to exist can create problems for the Democrats in this area.

Similarly, foreign policy does not have to be a divisive issue for the Democrats. If they can agree to abandon the attempt to win back conservative southern whites, Democrats will find a great deal of harmony on foreign policy issues. It is true that many lower-class Democrats are attracted to a policy emphasizing a strong defense, and this often puts them at odds with the dominant liberal wing of the party. But it is easy to overstate such divisions. One of the ironies of the Reagan Administration's perceived successes is that it has lessened public support for a continuing defense build-up. And the rapidly evolving situation in the former Soviet Union and Eastern Europe make traditional liberal foreign policy proposals of conciliation, negotiation, and concern for human rights more attractive among all segments of the population. Thus, for example, in 1989 Gallup found that only 16 percent of Democrats (the same proportion as Republicans) felt our military defense was not strong enough (63 percent felt it was fine as it was; 17 percent felt it was stronger than it needed to be). And income differences were also minimal. Those earning under $20,000 per year were the most supportive of the view that our defenses were not strong enough, but even among that group only 22 percent supported such a position.[25]

In addition, traditional lower-class Democratic groups are more liberal on foreign policy issues than observers often note. For example, in 1984, while a majority of white Protestants agreed that strengthening our defenses should take priority over negotiating a nuclear freeze with the Soviet Union, a majority of white Catholics had just the opposite priority.[26] And in February 1990, Gallup reported that only 22 percent of Democrats (compared with 34 percent of Republicans) felt we should ease sanctions against South Africa as a reward for that government's release of Nelson Mandela and continued "progress" in eliminating apartheid. (In addition, on this question there were no income differences: 25 percent of those earning under $20,000 favored easing sanctions; among those earning over $50,000, 27 percent supported such a move.)[27] Foreign policy proposals which concentrate on cooperation and human rights can bind the Democratic coalition together. There is no need for the Democrats to tie themselves up in knots trying to show they are tougher on defense than the Republicans (that is, no more Michael Dukakis in a tank!). The public thinks we are strong enough to defend our interests, and the Democrats should remind us that there is no need for overkill and that we should, therefore, turn our attention to domestic issues.

Thus, the Democratic coalition can be brought together with general appeals to economic fairness, a clean environment, better education, and a foreign policy based on cooperation and support for human rights. (In the final section of the book, I will examine how these general themes can be fashioned into a more specific appeal which can also help bring renewed public commitment to active government and build a long-term coalition supportive of Democratic principles.) But we also need to note that there are sources of tension within the Democratic coalition. Without an awareness of those sources and a strategy for alleviating (if not eliminating) them, Republicans will still be able to exploit Democratic divisions and hinder the party's attempt to rebuild itself.

Sources of Tension

The largest source of tension in the Democratic Party is the politics of race. Stanley Greenberg, a Democratic consultant, notes that "when the middle class thinks about car insurance, they think they're paying for people who are uninsured who they assume to be black or Puerto Rican"[28] Similarly, David Sears and Jack Citrin's study of California voters' feelings toward property taxes revealed that racism played a major role in shaping attitudes on that seemingly unrelated economic issue. In analyzing these results, they concluded:

> The blunt truth is that race remains a central issue in American domestic politics, as it has been virtually throughout American history. It plays a powerful role in the public's decisions even on issues with no manifest racial content and in campaigns with relatively little explicit reference to race, as in the case of the tax revolt. Large numbers of whites remain fundamentally opposed to special government efforts to aid blacks, and that opposition was a central determinant of white support for the tax revolt.[29]

And there are differences of opinion between black and white Americans on a number of crucial issues involving civil rights. For example, in looking at the conditions that exist today, 45 percent of black Americans do not think there is equal opportunity in housing markets and 33 percent do not think there is equal educational opportunity. In contrast, only 23 percent of white Americans think housing markets discriminate, and only 13 percent think educational discrimination is a problem. And only 31 percent of all Democrats supported a 1988 Supreme Court decision upholding the legality of some affirmative action programs.

(The racial breakdown on the Supreme Court decision was 45 percent of blacks in support and only 22 percent of whites.) Similarly, a June 1991 Gallup survey found that 58 percent of white Americans felt we already had enough laws to combat racial discrimination (34 percent felt we needed more such laws), while only 30 percent of black Americans felt current law was adequate (62 percent wanted more laws). And 78 percent of black Americans felt companies should be required to hire employees in proportion to the racial make-up of the local community. Only 41 percent of white Americans felt this way.[30]

The public, particularly white Americans, is very skeptical of the need for policies especially targeted to help minority groups. But the importance of African-American voters within the Democratic coalition and the traditional commitment of the Democratic Party for social justice lead to support for such policies by the Democrats. This creates tension within their coalition. Issues of race, so long as they are seen as "us" against "them," are very divisive to the Democrats. Jesse Jackson's attempt to build a "rainbow" coalition was an attempt to cut through this tension and show the common ground that lower- and middle-class black and white (and other) citizens have. Although he failed to win the Democratic nomination, Jackson's ability to broaden his base of support from 1980 and 1984 shows some of the potential for such a strategy in the long run. Still, the Democrats need to deal more effectively with the divisiveness of the race issue. Recognition that the problems stem from a perception on the part of many white voters (especially lower- and middle-class white voters) that the Democrats do "too much" for minority groups and that those groups are getting an unfair advantage (perceptions obviously not shared by black voters)—and *not* from perceptions that blacks do not deserve equal treatment or that those in trouble do not deserve help—can help the Democrats fashion policies which can unite the party, not divide it on racial grounds.

Furthermore, the Democrats can work to educate the public as to the extent of racism still present in American society. Reports like those on ABC's *Primetime* show, which documented the different treatment accorded blacks and whites in housing, shopping and employment, can help make clear the continuing existence of racial discrimination.[31] Such awareness can help build support for policies to combat discrimination. It will not end tension over race issues. As long as the public, in part, sees these issues as "us against them," that tension will persist. The Democrats, need, therefore, to focus on the kinds of policies which can improve the situation of poor and middle class blacks and whites. (I will look more closely at such policies in Part Three of the book.)

Issues such as affirmative action and Israeli support for the government in South Africa, and charges of black antisemitism and Jewish racism have also fueled tension between two primary groups in the Democratic coalition, blacks and Jews. This tension is particularly noticeable in New York City (the one place in the country where both groups are large enough so that they both seem essential to Democratic chances for victory). There is no doubt that Jewish concern over "quotas" combined with black support for affirmative action programs creates legitimate policy differences between these two groups. But part of the "tension" is a function of bad politics on both sides. And the division between black and Jewish voters is as much myth as reality. Jesse Jackson's statements in the 1980 presidential campaign and Ed Koch's statements in the 1984 New York presidential primary fanned flames that do not need to exist. Jewish voters are the group of white voters most likely to support black candidates. When Harold Washington was first elected Mayor of Chicago, for example, Jewish voters gave him strong support (even though his Republican opponent, Bernard Epton, was Jewish). Jewish voters are still much more liberal on most social issues (and therefore, much more supportive of strong civil rights policies) than other white Americans. Similarly, black voters are at least as supportive of Israel as white voters,[32] and the Congressional Black Caucus contains some of Congress's strongest supporters of Israel. There is tension in the Democratic Party over issues of race, but in general Jewish voters are more likely to be allied with African-American voters than are other white Democrats.

A second source of tension for the Democrats is the question of taxes. The perceived unfairness of the tax laws often results in less support among usually Democratic groups for raising revenues to pay for social programs. In October 1988, for example, Gallup found that while 75 percent of those earning over $40,000 a year were willing to pay higher taxes to raise educational standards, only 52 percent of those earning under $10,000 were willing to do so. (Note that even here, however, there is majority support.)[33] Republican appeals on the tax issue, then, can cut into the Democratic coalition so long as the tax structure is seen as unfair and lower- and middle-class citizens feel they will have to pay more than their fair share of any increases. But it is important to remember (as we saw in chapter 4) that this opposition is not an objection to taxes per se or an objection to greater government involvement. Rather, it is motivated by perceptions of the fairness of the tax system. Rebuilding trust in government, pursuing policies that make government important to middle-class as well as poor Americans, and making the tax system fairer can all help to overcome the divisiveness that this issue creates.

Social issues such as crime, the death penalty, and abortion furnish the third major source of tension in the Democratic coalition. As we saw in Chapter 3, however, these issues need not be as divisive as they sometimes appear. In the case of abortion, as we have seen, the issue is likely to be more of a problem for Republicans than Democrats, so long as Democrats can keep the issue focused on who should be making the choice about abortion, individual women or the government. It is also important to note in this regard that Catholic opinion on the abortion issue is no different from Protestant opinion. (Jewish voters are substantially more liberal on abortion than either Catholics or Protestants.) Thus, for example, in April 1990, Gallup found that 28 percent of Protestants felt that abortions should always be legal, 56 percent felt that abortion should be legal under some circumstances, and 12 percent felt they should never be legal. Among Catholics the figures were an almost identical 29 percent always legal, 55 percent sometimes legal, and 13 percent never legal. (Among Jewish voters, in contrast, 62 percent felt they should always be legal.)[34] The very visible opposition to legal abortion by the Catholic Church often obscures the relative support for legal abortion among Catholic laypeople. Mario Cuomo's position that he does not personally condone abortion but that it is a decision that individuals of differing religious beliefs should decide for themselves, not be dictated by government, is more in line with Catholic opinion on the issue than is the official Church view that abortion should only be allowed in cases where the life of the mother is in danger.

In other areas of social policy, there is some tendency for lower-income Americans to be more conservative than higher-income Americans. For example, George Bush was able to make strong appeals to working-class Democrats in 1988 by raising the issue of Dukakis's support for early release and parole programs for convicted criminals (the Willie Horton case). But as noted in Chapter 3, the Democrats' problems in this area have more to do with image than with specific policy proposals. These policies are not seen as "important policies" by most people. It is the way the Republicans use the Democrats' positions to portray them as "weak" that is the problem. Thus, even where the public does oppose Democratic positions, such as the death penalty, such opposition need not be fatal to the Democrats.

Furthermore, there are, as we have seen, a number of crime related issues where the Democrats can gain public support. Gun control is the most obvious of these areas. For example, 73 percent of Democrats (and Republicans!) support banning assault rifles (according to a March 1989 Gallup survey). And while there are some income-related differences, with "only" 66 percent of those earning under $15,000 in support of such a ban compared with 76 percent of those with family incomes over $40,000, support tends to run across all groups of the Democratic coalition. (Catholics, for example, showed 74 percent support of such action). An August 1988 Gallup Poll found that 69 percent of Democrats wanted to make laws concerning handguns more strict (compared with 60 percent of Republicans). Again, there were some income differences. In families with incomes under $15,000, support for stricter laws was 58 percent, while for those with family incomes over $40,000 support was at 69 percent.[35] Issues of crime (and other social issues) need not seriously divide the Democratic coalition, particularly if the Democrats understand that the differences that do emerge are more related to perceptions of image or style (or to underlying racial tensions) than to actual policy differences.

Finally, issues of defense and foreign policy are often cited as divisive among Democrats. But as noted earlier, much of this divisiveness will disappear when the Democrats give up trying to win back conservative southern whites. When that group is left out of the equation, foreign policy issues which focus on international cooperation and human rights can unify Democratic constituencies. The Democrats still need to be concerned about the potential divisiveness of defense and foreign policy issues if the party's image of being "too weak" on defense issues remains salient. But as with the crime issue, this image problem is only tangentially related to specific policy proposals. The Democrats need to address these problems, but not by backing away from liberal, progressive stands.

Conclusion

There is, then, the raw material to rebuild the Democratic New Deal coalition. The rebuilt coalition will not be identical to the Roosevelt coalition. In particular, the affluent conservative, southern white segment of the coalition should be jettisoned, and upper middle class women and the growing Hispanic population should be added to the coalition. And issues of economic fairness and redistribution need to be supplemented with appeals for social justice, a cleaner environment, and a foreign policy based on cooperation and human rights. Such a general platform can unite this revised Democratic coalition. At the same time the Democrats need to deal with the divisive (or potentially divisive) ef-

Table 6-3

Democrats' Closeness to Dukakis and Bush (in percent)

Policy Area	Dukakis	Don't Know or Both	Neither	Bush
Support for Homeless	63	28	3	6
Health Care	60	29	2	9
Public Education	57	33	1	9
The Environment	54	35	2	9
The Deficit	57	30	3	10
Day Care	52	39	2	7
Tax Policy	54	32	3	11
Drugs	55	33	3	9
Defense Policy	52	28	3	17
Foreign Policy	46	33	2	19
The Death Penalty	34	54	3	9

Percentage is the percentage of Democrats who felt their own position on the appropriate issue was closer to Dukakis or Bush.
Source: *The Gallup Report*, May 1988, pp. 9–19.

fects of issues such as toughness on crime and in defense policy, too much taxation, and, especially, race. The potential of this type of approach for unifying the Democratic Party can be seen in the results of a May 1988 Gallup survey. The survey asked potential voters whether George Bush or Michael Dukakis had policy positions closer to their own on a variety of issues. Table 6-3 shows the responses of Democrats to these questions. As can be seen, the unifying effect of issues such as care for the homeless, health care, public education, the environment, the deficit, day care, and drugs is great. Over half the Democrats said they were closer to Dukakis and fewer than 10 percent said they were closer to Bush (the rest said they were equally close to both or close to neither). And tax policy was almost as unifying with 54 percent closer to Dukakis, and 11 percent saying they were closer to Bush. Only the areas of defense, foreign policy, and the death penalty showed strong potential for divisiveness, as fair numbers of Democrats preferred George Bush or, in the case of the death penalty, only a small number supported the Dukakis position.

A major study done in 1988 by Gallup for the Times Mirror Corporation confirms these trends. The Times Mirror study looked in great detail at the values and opinions of a large sample of the American public.[36] It found that nine basic values drive and divide the American public: religious faith (or the lack thereof), attitudes of tolerance, views on social justice, level of support for militant anticommunism, degree of alienation, views on American exceptionalism, degree of financial pressure individuals felt, attitudes toward government, and attitudes toward big business. Various combinations of these attitudes led the researchers to classify Americans in eleven different groups, two of which are predominately Republican, five of which are predominately independent (two of which lean Democratic), and four of which are Democratic.[37]

The four Democratic groups, according to the Times Mirror survey, are:

1. The "60s Democrats" (who make up 8 percent of the population but 11 percent of the electorate): This group has a strong commitment to social justice, a clean environment, civil rights, and social spending. It also tends to oppose military spending.

2. New Deal Democrats (11 percent of the population but 15 percent of the electorate): This group also favors social spending, but not if it seems targeted at minorities. It tends to be more conservative on abortion than the 60s Democrats, and it strongly supports protectionist economic policies to protect American jobs.

3. The Passive Poor (7 percent of the population but only 6 percent of the electorate): This group tends to support all social spending, but it is more supportive of defense spending than 60s Democrats. It also is the least supportive of the Democratic groups for strong environmental policies.

4. The Partisan Poor (9 percent of the population and the electorate): This group is strongly supportive of social justice and social spending of all kinds. It, like the 60s Democrats, wants

to reduce military spending, but it tends to be more supportive of tougher action on crime and more conservative on
social issues than that group.

In looking more closely at these divisions, Ornstein, Kohut,
and McCarthy note "attitudes toward social justice—a concept
encompassing beliefs about welfarism, egalitarianism and racial
equality—to be the single factor that most differentiates those in
the solidly Republican clusters from those in the solidly Democratic clusters." [38]

Furthermore, the study found that opinions about social justice
related to candidate preferences more strongly than any other
political value in the study. Thus, as I have indicated here, policies concerned with making American society more just, fair,
and egalitarian, the kinds of policies associated with and supported by the progressive, liberal wing of the Democratic party,
hold strong unifying potential for the party. The policy areas of
strongest Democratic agreement are support for trade policies to
protect American jobs, increases in federal spending—particularly in the areas of health care, drug addiction, education, and
helping the homeless—and a reluctance to risk U.S. military involvement abroad.[39] The study reached the heartening conclusion
that "Democratic divisions are not being aggravated by foreign
policy issues."[40]

Similarly, the study found the strongest divisive area for the
Democrats was "spending for the middle class versus spending
for the poor," which turns out to be, largely, a function of the
race issue. New Deal Democrats, in particular, are less supportive of spending targeted toward minority groups than other Democratic blocs.[41]

In the end, then, the Democratic coalition can be rebuilt
around the issues of social justice and a fairer and more egalitarian society. The race issue is a problem, and so is the tendency of
the public, noted in Part One of the book, to distrust government
programs and to feel alienated from the system. But the raw
materials are present. If the Democrats can overcome the politics

of race (particularly as an "us" against "them" issue), rebuild public confidence in public institutions (certainly no easy task), and promote policies that are beneficial not only to the poor but also to middle-class voters, then there is the potential for the Democrats to put together a strong, progressive governing coalition. In the final part of the book, I will, finally, explore in more detail just how the Democratic Party can achieve this goal. But before we do that, we need to examine the Republican coalition and its strengths and weaknesses, for only then can we fully understand the possibilities that exist for the Democratic Party.

7

The Republicans: United Right?

In order to understand fully the dynamics of building a Democratic coalition, we also need to understand the forces that unify and divide the Republican coalition. The Reagan years have seen growth in the number of self-identified Republicans (although Democrats still outnumber Republicans by a 4-to-3 margin), and continued Republican success in presidential elections, usually by large if not landslide proportions, give the perception of a Republican resurgence. But the inability of the Republican Party to turn its continuing success at the presidential level into control of Congress or a lead in party identification has been frustrating to the party. And the landslide victories of Ronald Reagan and comfortable win of George Bush mask a good deal of division within Republican ranks.

The Republican Coalition

The core of the Republican coalition since the New Deal has been and still is, upper and upper middle-class Protestant voters (outside of the South). In 1984, Ronald Reagan received 68 percent of the vote of people in families with over $50,000 per year in income, 71 percent of the vote of white Anglo-Saxon Protestants, and 68 percent of the vote among households headed by business people or professionals.[1] Similarly, in 1988 George Bush received 70 percent of the vote of people in families with annual incomes over $50,000, 66 percent of the votes of white Protestants, and 62 percent of the vote of those households whose head of household was a manager.[2]

This traditional Republican base is attracted to the party largely on the basis of economic issues. The Republicans have long been seen as the best party for the interests of business. Martin Wattenberg, for example, notes that the 1960 National Election Study found that the public felt by a 42 percent to 15 percent margin the Republicans and not the Democrats were the party most likely to leave things to private business, and that a 1985 *New York Times* poll found that 66 percent of the electorate considered the Republicans the party that cared most about the needs and problems of big business (17 percent said the Democrats cared more). As he comments: "It should come as no surprise that those who identified with business people were among Reagan's and Bush's strongest supporters."[3]

Traditionally, there has been some tension within this group of Republicans between "Wall Street" and "Main Street." The Wall Street wing of the party has been seen as more internationalist in foreign policy and liberal on social issues than the Main Street wing. But the unity of the party on economic issues was, and is, clear.

Since the 1960s, however, this traditional economically conservative, high-income, northern and western Protestant base has been supplemented by two other groups, whom Wattenberg calls the "New Right" and the "Democratic Right." The Democratic Right is the old Democratic South. This is the group of voters who, as we saw in the last chapter, has left the Democratic Party, at least at the presidential level, in part over issues of race and in part over economic issues. As noted, the loyalty of upper-income Protestants in the South to the Democratic Party was always an anomaly anyway. Once torn from the Democratic coalition as a result of the race issue, these voters have found their economic interests better represented by the Republican Party than they had been by the Democrats (at least at the national level).

The other group that has moved to support the Republicans in recent years is religious fundamentalists, often called the New Right. Many of these voters are also in the South. In fact, in looking at the "conversion" of the white South to the Republican Party in presidential elections, it is important to recognize two distinct movements into the Republican Party: one of upper-class whites, the other of lower-class religious fundamentalist white voters. While the race issue may have led both groups to question their allegiance to the Democrats, their reasons for supporting Republicans are very different. The former group, as noted above, finds their economic interests best served by the Republicans. For the latter group, however, it is the social and moral conservatism of the Republican Party that is so attractive. The fundamentalist right supports the Republicans out of a desire for conservative policies in matters of morality and traditional family values. Concern about a decay in the moral fiber of America as seen, for example, in the rise of homosexuality, the legality of abortion, and the use of drugs is what pushes this group into the Republican Party. And they now make up a large element in the Republican coalition. The 1988 *New York Times* exit poll found that white fundamentalists made up about 10 percent of the electorate and that this group voted 81 percent Republican. (As Wattenberg notes, this situation is very similar to that of black voters in the Democratic coalition. Black voters also make up 10 percent of the electorate, and they voted, according to the *New York Times*, 86 percent Democratic).[4]

Thus, the core of the Republican coalition is traditional upper- and upper-middle-class white voters combined with fundamentalist Christians. There has, however, been some movement among Catholic and working-class voters as well. While these groups have not deserted the Democratic Party, as discussed in Chapter 6, they have moved in a Republican direction. Larry Sabato notes: "many other blocs that remain outside the GOP orbit, including blue-collar workers and Roman Catholics, are much less monolithically Democratic than they once were."[5]

As we shall see, the attraction of these formerly solid Democratic groups toward the Republican Party seems to reflect four issues: taxes, trust in government, moral or social conservatism and defense/foreign policy concerns. In all four areas, the position of the Republican Party as more conservative (that is, opposing taxes, not trusting government, defending "traditional moral values," and wanting a strong defense) has cut into the Democratic loyalty of these groups.

Additionally, there are two other factors which help the Republican coalition. Republican voters vote more often than Democrats, and they are much more loyal than Democrats. Both of these factors have been true since at least the Eisenhower years. Republicans have always been able to count on support from at least 90 percent of their supporters, while Democrats have been somewhat less loyal. Table 7-1 shows the loyalty of white voters to their parties in presidential voting since 1952. As can be seen, even in the Johnson landslide of 1964, 91 percent of "strong" Republicans were loyal. Democrats, on the other hand, suffered defections as high as 34 percent in 1972. Even in 1988, Republicans were slightly more loyal than Democrats (98 percent to 93 percent). Similarly, Sabato found that 36 percent of Democratic identifiers in 1986 felt "somewhat estranged" from their party, compared with just 16 percent of Republicans.[6]

Republican voters are also more likely to vote. In 1988, for example, according to the National Election Vote Validation Study (which checks voting records to see if people actually did vote), 76 percent of "strong" Republicans went to the polls compared with 68 percent of Democrats. (The figures for "weak" partisans were 54 percent of Democrats and 63 percent of Republicans).[7]

The relative homogeneity of the Republican coalition (it is, after all, basically just two groups, as opposed to the more divided Democratic coalition) and the loyalty of Republican voters, both in terms of willingness to vote and to support their party, are barriers to Democratic dominance. There are, however, important

Table 7-1

Loyalty of Party Identifiers and Leaners, 1952–1988 (in percent)

Party Identification	1952	1956	1960	1964	1968	1972	1976	1980	1984	1988
Strong Democrat	82	85	91	94	89	66	88	87	88	93
Weak Democrat	61	63	70	81	66	44	72	59	63	68
Ind. Lean Democratic	60	65	89	89	62	58	73	57	77	86
Ind. Lean Republican	93	94	87	75	95	89	85	87	95	87
Weak Republican	96	93	89	60	90	81	78	95	94	84
Strong Republican	98	99	98	91	97	98	97	96	98	98

Percentage is the percentage of each group supporting its party's presidential candidate.

Source: American National Election Studies. Adapted from Abramson, Paul, John Aldrich, and David Rohde, *Change and Continuity in the 1988 Elections*, p. 211.

cracks in the Republican coalition. But before we look at the factors that do, in fact, divide Republicans, we need to take a closer look at the issues which bring them together.

Sources of Cohesion

The changing nature of the Republican coalition, as poorer, white evangelical Christians have joined, has given the party less unity on economic issues than was once the case. But there still are some economic issues which unite it, the most important of which is the tax issue. The Republicans have always been seen as the party that is less willing to raise taxes, and that image attracts not only upper-income Americans but also many middle- and working-class Americans who feel that they pay more than their fair share of taxes. George Bush's famous "read my lips, no new taxes" pledge, and the uproar among conservative Republicans when he backed away from the pledge in the fall 1990 budget negotiations, are two signs of the importance of this issue to the Republicans.

As we saw in Chapter 4, however, much of the dissatisfaction with taxes is a belief in the unfairness of the system, not an opposition to taxes in general. Still, that belief in unfairness is widespread. When evaluating the Tax Reform Act of 1986, for example, only 13 percent of the public felt the law had made the tax system fairer, while 39 percent felt it made things less fair (33 percent felt it made no difference, and 15 percent did not know what effect it had). And while perceptions differ somewhat according to income, with 46 percent of those with annual family incomes of over $50,000 feeling the reforms made the system less fair compared with only 35 percent of those earning under $15,000 per year feeling that way, those differences are not large. People across the board find taxes to be unfair and are skeptical of efforts to raise them. Thus, when asked to choose whether a tax increase, a rise in prices, an increase in interest rates, or the loss of a job for the individual or a spouse created more worries, 42 percent choose the tax increase. (The second most common response was an increase in prices, selected by 24 percent.)[8] This widespread distrust of the tax system helps keep the Republican coalition together. As we shall see, however, the perception that the system is unfair in part because the wealthy do not pay their fair share can be used by Democrats promoting more progressive taxes to turn the tax issue against the Republicans.

Distrust of government's ability to solve problems also binds Republicans together. As noted earlier, there is a widespread perception that government is often more of a problem than a solution. While people want government to do things in the abstract, they are skeptical of the ability of any particular program to work. Thus, in June 1985 Gallup found that 50 percent of the public felt big government was more of a threat than either big business or big labor.[9] Republican appeals to "stop throwing money at problems," and reminders of the need to eliminate "waste or abuse" help draw the party together. The Democrats, I have argued, need to address both the issue of fairness in the tax structure and the problem of people's trust in government if they are going to build a long-term governing coalition.

Republicans also have found unity on defense and foreign policy issues.[10] In particular, the need to maintain a strong defense against the Soviet threat and the dangers of communism have always been a force that bound different strands of American conservatism together. And in the late 1970s and early 1980s, Ronald Reagan and other conservative Republicans were able to draw much support from their calls for increased defense spending. But as noted in Chapter 6, in many ways the perceived success of Reagan in strengthening our defenses has weakened that appeal. Similarly, the democratization of Eastern Europe, destruction of the USSR, and end of the Cold War have given such appeals less strength. Still, the commitment to a strong defense is something that tends to unite Republicans.

Issues of race also tend to unify the Republican Party. The party does not have any constituency at all among black voters and a very limited one among Hispanic voters and thus feels none of the cross-pressures that the Democrats experience. Since at least 1968, Republicans have consciously tried to exploit aspects of the racial tension within the Democratic Party to win both southern and northern working-class whites into their party. In particular, they have employed calls for "law and order," calls which are often understood as appeals to stop the black criminals who, some feel, are making our cities unsafe. (Remember Willie Horton.) Similarly, Republicans through their opposition to affirmative action programs have exploited the perception of many working class whites that black Americans are given "special privileges."

I do not mean to imply that all opposition to affirmative action is racially motivated. There are other reasons one might oppose affirmative action programs. But to many white middle-class Americans, this is an issue of "fairness," and their perception is that black and other minority Americans are being given an unfair advantage. (Recall also the image that people have of the Democratic Party as siding too much with minorities.) "They have an advantage that we do not" is the way that many whites see this issue. Thus, Republican opposition to such programs appeals to many middle- and working-class white voters, as well as to more traditional upper-class Republican voters, whose opposition also reflects a desire to avoid government interference in private industry.

There are also several social issues on which the public clearly supports the Republican Party's position. Most visible in recent elections have been the death penalty, prayer in school, and flag-burning. The public strongly advocates the use of the death penalty. A 1986 Gallup survey which asked people to choose between the death penalty and life imprisonment without parole as the penalty for murder found that 55 percent chose the death penalty and 35 percent chose life imprisonment. More importantly, Republicans chose the death penalty by a 68-to-24 percent margin, while Democrats showed strong divisions, with 47 percent choosing the death penalty and 43 percent choosing life imprisonment without parole.[11] Similarly, public support for school prayer is strong. Seventy percent of the public supported a return of prayer to the schools in a 1988 Gallup survey (72 percent of Republicans).[12] Furthermore, the *New York Times* cited a 1989 survey which indicated that 69 percent of the public supported a constitutional amendment to ban flag burning.[13]

Finally, the Republicans have been united, in recent years, by the perception that Ronald Reagan was a successful President who got the country's economy in order. Thus, in 1984 58 percent of the public approved of Ronald Reagan's handling of the economy, and 86 percent of those people supported him for re-election. In 1988, 54 percent of the public approved of Reagan's handling of the economy, and 80 percent of those people voted for George Bush.[14] Similarly, in 1984, 63 percent of the public approved of the way Ronald Reagan was handling his job as President, and of that number 87 percent supported him for re-election; while in 1988, the percentage approving of Reagan's handling of the Presidency stood at 60 percent with 79 percent of them voting for George Bush.[15]

Thus, the Republican Party can rely on a number of themes and issues to promote party unity. In particular, distrust of government solutions, dissatisfaction with the tax system, the need for a strong defense, opposition to "giving an unfair advantage" to minority groups, and appeal to the legacy of the Reagan years can help bring the party together. But there are also a number of forces which tend to pull the Republican Party apart.

Sources of Division

The popularity of Ronald Reagan and the perception of his success helped to mask many of the divisions within the Republican Party. The most important of these are the major differences between traditional upper-income Republicans and white evangelical Christian Republicans. The social issue agenda of the latter group is either not important to, or actually opposed by, the former group. Nowhere is this seen more clearly than the abortion issue. The strong opposition of the Christian Right to legalized abortions is clear. On the other hand, many upper income, well-educated Republicans (especially Republican women), support a pro-choice policy. According to a 1990 Gallup survey, only 9 percent of those with college degrees want to make all abortions illegal, and only 8 percent of those with family incomes of over $50,000 support such a position. On the other hand, 17 percent of those without a high school degree and 13 percent of those with family incomes under $20,000 support outlawing abortion.[16]

As long as the Supreme Court kept overturning laws to restrict abortion, the Republican Party had it easy on this issue. It could take a strong anti-abortion position, calling for laws to limit the practice, satisfying its socially conservative followers. At the same time, the protection afforded by the courts to women who desired an abortion meant that pro-choice, upper-income Republicans did not have to worry if they were supporting right-to-life candidates. The Supreme Court made that a moot issue. (This was especially true because there never was enough anti-abortion sentiment to make the prospect of a constitutional amendment banning abortions anything more than an abstract threat.) But the Court's signal in the *Webster* case[17] that it would uphold more restrictions on abortion and, perhaps, even consider overturning the 1973 *Roe v. Wade* decision which legalized abortion has changed all that. Voting for right-to-life Republicans no longer seems so abstract. The defection of upper-class Republicans over the abortion issue is potentially an important problem for the party. Such defections certainly helped Democrat Douglas Wilder win the Virginia governor's race in 1989 and were also a factor in the election of James Florio as Governor of New Jersey in 1989 and Ann Richards as Governor of Texas in 1990 (an election which showed an enormous gender gap). The Republican Party has been scrambling to find new ground on the issue. George Bush's appeal for a "big tent" in the Republican Party on the abortion issue has been one attempt to stem the divisions this issue is causing within Republican ranks.

But the divisions between these two groups of Republicans runs deeper than simply the abortion issue. For conservative white evangelical Christians, the major issues are social issues. The decline of "traditional American values" is, in their mind, the most serious problem facing the nation, and they want government to pursue a strong, interventionist policy in social areas. Government action against pornography and obscenity, the reintroduction of school prayer, fighting the perceived growth of homosexuality, and banning abortion make up just a part of a broad agenda that this group would like to see enacted. But strong government action in this (or any) area tends to run counter to the inclination of upper-income, better-educated Republicans. Even if they do not generally oppose this conservative agenda, they do not see it as a top priority. And at times, as in the case of abortion and government funding for the arts (which to the Christian Right is an issue of funding pornography), there is strong opposition to this agenda. The Mapplethorpe case in Cincinnati, in which the Director of the Cincinnati Museum of Art was accused of distributing pornography for bringing an exhibit of the photographs of Robert Mapplethorpe to the museum, also points to these divisions. Wealthy Republican patrons of the arts are not attracted to an agenda which interferes with the ability of museums to display art.

In fact, certain policies supported by upper-income Republicans have come under attack by the Christian Right as interfering with "traditional family values." Policies such as improving sex education (including discussions of AIDS), providing equal opportunities for women outside the home, and, especially, improving child care options are often seen by conservative evangelicals as attacks on the family. But such policies are popular among better-educated, higher-income Republicans. The child care issue, in particular, is one where Democratic support for more action can force the Republicans into making uncomfortable choices which are likely to alienate large numbers of their supporters. As Martin Wattenberg noted,

> The New and Old Right are clearly at odds with each other on social issues such as abortion, school prayer, and equal rights for women. When economic times are not particularly favorable toward the Republicans, the social issue agenda of fundamentalist Christians may prove to be a significant source of alienation to upper-income voters.[18]

In addition, the evangelical wing of the Republican Party is not, in general, as adverse to social spending and government activity as are traditional Republicans. They do, as noted above, share a skepticism of government and a dislike of taxes, but they also support government provision of many services and programs, particularly if those programs are not seen as catering to the interests of minorities. In this case, their economic interests bring them more in line with Democratic policies than with Republican reliance on the private sector.

As we saw in Chapter 3, the public's distrust of big business is at least as great as its distrust of big government. When Roper asked whether big business needed to be watched by government or could be trusted to follow "fair" policies on its own, the public overwhelming supported the position that government needed to keep an eye on business. For example, on the issue of cleaning up the air and water pollution created by business, 88 percent of the public felt government needs to keep an eye on business, while only 12 percent felt business would take responsibility on its own. Similarly, only 14 percent of the public felt business would not illegally fix prices if left on their own, only 22 percent felt business would make their products and services safe, only 27 percent felt business would advertise honestly, and only 29 percent felt business would provide safe working conditions. The only area where over a third of the public trusted business if left on its own was hiring without discrimination, and even there support for business was only at 37 percent. The other 63 percent of the public felt government needed to keep an eye on business.[19]

The Republican coalition is particularly vulnerable to division over environmental issues, particularly the need for strict governmental controls of business and industry in order to clean up our air and water. As noted in the last chapter, such issues also create some splits between working-class Democrats worried about the effects of such controls on jobs and more socially liberal Democrats, but they create even more tension between better-educated environmentally conscious Republicans and business interests within the Republican Party who fight any such controls. Republicans feel much more cross-pressure between constituent support for stronger environmental action and business opposition to such policies than do Democrats. Thus, Gallup found that the percentage of Republicans who thought of themselves as environmentalists was almost identical to the percentage of Democrats who felt that way (35 percent of Republicans called themselves "strong environmentalists" compared with 40 percent of Democrats; 39 percent of Republicans called themselves "not strong" environmentalists compared with 33 percent of Democrats), and more upper income than lower income individuals thought of themselves as environmentalists. (The figures: those with family incomes over $50,000: 35 percent strong environmentalists, 43 percent not strong environmentalists; those under $20,000: 34 percent strong environmentalists, 33 percent not strong environmentalists.)[20] Since the Republican Party tends to be more opposed to strict environmental controls than the Democratic, such figures indicate the divisive impact these issues can have on the Republican coalition.

Thus, concerning many of the traditional economic areas which have provided the core of support for the Republicans over the years, the influx of new, socially conservative Republicans has led to tension within the party. Moreover, changes in the foreign policy environment resulting from the breakup of the Soviet empire and the perception that United States defense spending is more than adequate make defense issues less binding than they had been in the Reagan years. The public is much more amenable now to Democratic arguments about the need to redirect resources from defense to domestic programs, and such arguments can pull at the Republican Party.

Conclusion

The Republican Party, then, also faces a difficult time keeping its coalition together. The transition from Ronald Reagan to George Bush removes one of the strong forces of unity that the party has had over the past decade, and if the country should slide into recession, a second source of unity—"success at handling the economy"—will also disappear. The more lasting sources of unity (for the economy cannot grow indefinitely) are the public's distrust of government and the perceptions of unfairness in the structure of taxes in this country. Republicans also tend to be united by a desire for a strong defense and by a distrust of programs that are seen as helping minorities at the expense of white Americans. Democrats need to address these issues in constructive and progressive ways.

On the other hand, there are also a large number of policy areas where the Democrats are more unified, and where the Republicans face divisions within their own ranks. Table 7-2 repeats the information shown in Table 6-3 but this time for Republicans. A comparison of the two tables indicates how much more divided the Republicans are on domestic policy issues. Whereas the Democrats were united on most issues, there were strong Republican defections (and/or low levels of support for

Table 7-2

Republicans' Closeness to Dukakis and Bush (in percent)

Policy Area	Dukakis	Don't Know or Both	Neither	Bush
Support for homeless	27	40	1	32
Health care	19	35	2	44
Public education	20	33	1	46
The environment	20	40	1	39
The deficit	15	27	4	54
Day care	20	49	1	30
Tax policy	15	30	0	55
Drugs	13	33	3	51
Defense policy	9	22	0	69
Foreign policy	9	20	1	70
The death penalty	7	55	1	37

Percentage is the percentage of Republicans who felt their own position on the appropriate issue was closer to Dukakis or Bush.

Source: *The Gallup Report*, May 1988, pp. 9–19.

the Bush position) in the areas of aid to the homeless, health care, education, the environment, the deficit, day care, tax policy, drugs, and the death penalty. Only on the issues of foreign and defense policy was Republican support overwhelmingly united. In all other areas, at least 10 percent (and in most cases more than 15 percent) of Republicans favored the position of Dukakis, and in many less than half said they were closer to George Bush's views.

The Times-Mirror survey cited at the end of the last chapter also supports the argument I have been making. It did find more social (though not necessarily policy) homogeneity among the Republicans than the Democrats. Where there are four groups of Democrats, there are only two groups of Republicans.[21] These groups are:

1. *Enterprise Republicans* (10 percent of the population but 16 percent of the likely electorate). These are the traditional, upper-income Republican supporters. They oppose spending

for health care and aid to the homeless and the elderly, and they also oppose abortion restrictions.

2. *Moral Republicans* (11 percent of the population but 14 percent of the likely electorate): These are strongly anti-abortion, anti-communist, socially conservative Republicans. They are pro-defense spending, but they do not always oppose social spending programs.

These groups, then, are united in their views on a number of social issues and foreign policy and defense issues. But as Ornstein, Kohut, and McCarthy note: "One area where the two solid GOP groups do not concur is on social spending. While the Enterprisers tend to oppose all increases in social spending, Moralists generally favor such spending unless it is specifically targeted to minorities. The groups are also divided on abortion."[22]

Thus, there are clear and important divisions among Republicans which the Democratic Party can exploit in areas such as social policy and the need for government activity to solve social problems. Discussing such issues by themselves will not cause major defections from the Republicans to the Democrats. But it will create tension within the Republican coalition and cause the kind of discomfort that the Democrats have felt when the Republicans have successfully exploited Democratic divisions over issues such as the death penalty or matters relating to race. Putting the Republican Party on the defensive and causing it to deal with its own internal struggles is one step the Democrats must take if they are to refocus public attention on an agenda more favorable to the Democratic Party. Additionally, the Democrats need to deal with those forces which unify the Republican Party, in particular the issues of taxes and distrust of government. I will now turn to a strategy which will help the Democrats do just that while simultaneously rebuilding a progressive governing coalition.

Part Three

Building a Progressive Democratic Party

8

Making Politics Matter Again: The Politics of Inclusion

Rebuilding the Democratic Party is a long-term task. It will not be accomplished overnight. But as we have seen, the raw materials are already in place to begin that rebuilding. The public, the conventional wisdom notwithstanding, has not moved to the right during the Reagan-Bush years. It is still operationally liberal and progressive. Liberal and progressive candidates have been victorious on a statewide level in many states, and the New Deal coalition, while altered, is still present at least in a skeletal form. But the Democrats do need to give people a reason to support them. They need to help people reconnect to politics and government; so doing will build support for a party that is dedicated to using government as a tool of the people to improve our quality of life and create a more fair and just society. Government cannot be "the problem" if progressive policies are to succeed. If the Democrats simply "move to the center" (that is, become less distinguishable from the Republicans), they will give people little reason to support them. Whatever one felt about Ronald Reagan and his policies, one thing that was always clear was what he stood for. He was not calling for the same things the Democrats wanted, and people liked that about him, even when they often disagreed with what he was calling for. Democrats must remember that lesson. They must build on the policies that distinguish them from the Republicans. And they must do so with policies that rebuild trust in the political process. In the first two parts of this book, we explored the state of public opinion in the United States in the early 1990s. I have argued that the raw materials do exist to build a progressive coalition in the United States. Now, finally, we need to look at how such a coalition can be put together. What approach can the Democrats use to rebuild support for popular government? For the Democrats, the task is two-fold. They must rebuild their party, and they must develop a program that will gain popular support. In this chapter, we will look at the political strategies that the Democrats should follow. In Chapter 9, we will turn to the task of party building.

Putting Trust in the People

As we have seen, the largest barrier to building a progressive coalition in the United States is the lack of trust that people have in government. In the abstract, people support the use of government to solve problems, but their view of actual policies is that government is filled with waste, fraud, and abuse. They do not trust the government to do the right thing, and consequently, calls to cut back on government spending are often met with widespread support. (Many people believe spending can be cut without harming the substance of programs they support.) The first task for the Democratic Party, therefore, is to rebuild trust in government.

One of the problems, however, in rebuilding such trust is that government is seen by so many people as remote and irrelevant to their everyday lives. "People in Washington" make decisions which intrude on their lives without understanding their situations. The public is much more likely to express support for local government than for the national government, and it is much more likely to feel that it can make a difference at the local level. This is not, I would argue, a misperception. During the 1960s, the left often put an emphasis on popular (and local) participation in the implementation of programs. That emphasis was often seen as a cause of the failure of some of these programs.[1] The problem, however, was not a reliance on local participation. It was the reliance on participation outside of local government. Community boards and hearings were established but in ways which bypassed local government structures. Such set-ups simply reinforced attitudes of distrust towards existing government structures. What the Democrats need to do, I would argue, is push for policies which allow for a great deal of local flexibility in implementation.

Leaving decisions up to local governments does two things. First, it will create greater incentive for local political organizing (a topic I will return to in Chapter 9). And second, it will return decisions to those units of government with which people are most likely to be able to feel connected. Allowing local governments to make decisions concerning implementation means giving people a chance to make decisions about their own lives. In the short run, that may mean that some localities do not pursue policies that are as "progressive" as the national Democratic Party might like. Still, I would argue the Democrats should try to avoid the temptation to disallow such choices. Democracy is a messy form of government. It means trusting the people, even if they sometimes make the wrong decisions. And in the long run, allowing the public to feel they have some say in the decisions that government makes can only enhance the prospects of the Democratic Party. Trust in government is essential to building support for progressive policies.

But to say that we need to leave flexibility in implementation to local governments is not enough. There are, clearly, some policy areas where such flexibility is impossible. And it is also essential that the money for programs be provided at the national level. The national government is much more likely to raise revenues in a progressive fashion than are state and local governments. (I will return to the issue of taxes shortly.) In what areas, then, might such an approach have benefits?

First, I would argue that the Democrats should push for a reinstitution of federal revenue sharing. They should push for the national government to provide a certain amount of money to state and local governments with practically no strings attached. (There should, of course, be restrictions against the use of any federal money in programs which discriminate on the basis of race, gender, ethnicity, or religion.) Some localities will choose to use such funds to cut local taxes. Others may use such funds for provision of police or fire services, or to clean the streets, or for new parks. It does not really matter. There are two important progressive goals that federal revenue sharing can enhance. First, as noted above, leaving decisions to local government is likely to enhance public connections with the political system. The public is likely to feel that it can make a difference when decisions are made by its local government officials. This also provides incentive for the Democratic Party to organize at the local level. When important decisions are made at the local level, people will feel more need to get involved.

Second, federal revenue sharing can provide a measure of redistribution of resources. Federal taxes are already more progressive than state and local taxes. (And I will argue shortly for increasing their progressivity even further.) But revenue sharing should be tied to population. That way, poorer communities will receive more in resources than is collected in taxes from them. Richer communities, with more local resources to supplement these funds, will pay out more in federal taxes than they get back. In that regard, I would also add an element of progressivity to the payout formula, giving more to communities whose median income falls below the national average. But even a formula tied strictly to population would involve some kind of wealth redistribution.

In addition to general revenue sharing, four other areas stand out as targets for programs where the federal government provides the funds (or most of the funds) and local governments make the decisions about implementation: child care, education, recycling, and crime/drugs.

In each of these areas the Democrats should push for programs which allow for local control over resources. Any progressive platform in the United States will want to promote greater access to child care, improved public education, a cleaner environment, and safer communities for people to live in. Providing resources for communities to take actions in these areas can only help advance a progressive, liberal agenda. For example, in the matter of child care, some communities may want to subsidize government-run centers. Others may want to provide funds for private centers which take in children of poorer parents. Still others may want to provide funds for upgrading equipment at existing centers; or pay higher salaries for child care workers to increase their retention rate; or provide incentives for employers to set up on-site day care facilities for workers. Some communities may not make "the best choices," but increasing the availability of child care in any form will help.

Similarly, we should allow local school boards greater discretion over how to spend federal education funds. (I will argue in Chapter 9 that rebuilding the Democratic Party at the local level means getting involved in local politics at all levels, including education politics.) And the need for recycling programs does not mean every community needs to implement the same kind of program. But encouraging recycling everywhere is an important policy goal. Finally, it is not a "conservative" policy to want to make communities a safe place to live. As we saw in Chapter 3, the public is very supportive of rehabilitation and education, as opposed to stricter law enforcement, as a way to solve the drug problem, but giving communities choices about how they spend such resources is not going to "subvert" progressivism. If we want people to trust the government, we need to trust the people. And that means giving them the means to make important decisions about life in the communities in which they live.

As we also saw in Chapter 3, the public does support progressive policies in the areas of education, child care, and crime. It supports using public resources to enhance opportunities and programs in these areas. It even expresses a willingness to pay higher taxes to improve programs. We should build on that support to push for new initiatives in these areas, but we can also use

these policies to help reconnect people with their local governments and empower them to make important decisions about
how to solve problems. In the long run, the establishment of
bonds between the public and its government is the most important resource that a progressive coalition can have. Returning decisions to local government in these areas is an important
progressive goal.

Building a Fair Society

The first goal of a progressive Democratic Party, then, should be
to return power and responsibility to the public via its local governments. But, as noted, there are also policy areas where the
Democrats need to push for national policies that will enhance
the quality of people's lives. Such policies would make for a
more fair and just society and again, they will serve to reconnect
people to government by using government as our collective
voice to make our nation a better place to live.

One such area is the environment. Public support for strong
environmental policy is clear. And, with the exception of areas of
local concern such as recycling, this is a policy area which requires national rules and standards. Cleaning up the part of the
Colorado River which runs through Colorado is of limited use if
industries in other states can still dump waste into the river.
Similarly, the emissions which enter the atmosphere in the industrial Midwest affect the quality of air in the Northeast. And the
costs of cleaning up toxic waste dumps should not be borne only
by those who happen to live nearby. The Democratic Party
should support strong measures to clean up the environment.

There is, as we have seen, however, sometimes a problem for
the Democrats in this area. Strong environmental regulations can,
in the short run, lead to a loss of jobs, and thus such policies can
at times divide the Democratic coalition. On the other hand, as
we have also seen, most people do in fact support strong environmental policy. The Democrats must be clear to link such policies
with short-term help for those who might suffer economic hard-

ship (through, for example, job training programs or extended unemployment benefits). It is important to remind people of the consequences of environmental lapses. Public support is broad enough so that such policies are not likely to be as disruptive to the Democratic coalition as sometimes suggested. Similarly, these policies divide the Republican coalition at least as much as they divide the Democratic coalition. (Hence, George Bush's claim to be an "environmentalist.") The environment is an area where progressive policies will gain more public support than it will lose. A cleaner, safer environment enhances the quality of people's lives, and the Democrats should push for stronger measures in that regard.

In a similar fashion, the Democrats should push for policies which will improve the day-to-day lives of people. Affordable housing, something quickly moving beyond the reach of many young couples, access to higher education, and quality day care are three clear issues where the Democrats can promote government policy to help people directly in their lives. As argued above, the implementation of some of these policies should be left to local governments. But it is important for the Democratic Party to push for such policies. People need to be reconnected with government and its usefulness as a way to improve our collective lives. After the Second World War, veterans' benefits through the GI Bill and VHA loans made higher education and affordable housing a reality for millions of Americans. But in the 1980s, people are much less likely to find public help in these areas. For much of the middle class, the programs which exist are ones which their taxes pay for, but for which they are not eligible. The Democrats should not abandon their support for programs to help the poor. But they need to reconstruct the bonds of positive government for the middle class as well. Broad-based policies to improve access to housing, education, and child care are important tools in that regard.

Health care is another area where the Democrats need to push for more comprehensive national policy. The system as it has developed is a disaster from a standpoint of efficiency as well as equity. Tens of millions of Americans have no health insurance at all, and well over twenty million others are part of an inferior Medicaid system. In health care, one's ability to pay determines the kinds of medical treatment one gets, something which most Americans do not think of as fair. On the other hand, the hospitals and doctors who treat poor, uninsured, or Medicaid patients have to compete with profit-making hospitals that can offer higher-priced, more comprehensive care for those either with access to quality private insurance or the money to pay for services themselves. And such competition simply drains resources out of the public health system. A comprehensive public health insurance system would be more equitable and is also likely to be more efficient than the jury-rigged system we currently have, where doctors and patients spend more time filling out forms and checking on eligibility, reimbursement rates, and the like than either would care to. Currently, patients are often made to feel defensive about their status, and doctors often find it impossible to understand, let alone follow, the rules. Having a single set of health care rules for all citizens not only makes for more equity, it makes for a clearer public perception of the way in which government can improve the quality of public life. A health care system like social security, designed for all people whether they "need it" or not, would help build public support for positive government. Certainly, there would be strong opposition to such a policy from the American Medical Association and the Republican Party. But there is, as we have seen, a strong public perception that the current system is not working, and the Democrats should use that perception to push for comprehensive changes.

Another area where national reform is needed is welfare. I have argued that it is important to leave certain decisions to local government so that the public will feel connected to its government. However, welfare, like the environment, is an area which does not lend itself to local policy making, at least in terms of funding levels. If welfare funding decisions are made at the local level, all the incentives for local government are to have "bad" benefit programs. If a local government spends more money than neighboring states or localities, it provides incentive for people to move to that locality to receive those benefits. (People are unlikely to move across the country to improve the quality of their welfare benefits, but if they are choosing between living in New York or New Jersey, say, such choices are possible.) A good, comprehensive policy is expensive, and the states most likely to need such programs are those least likely to be able to afford them (because they have more poor people). Clearly, there are differences in the cost of living around the nation, so we do not need a program with uniform payment rules. And local governments can tailor their particular programs to local needs and concerns, so that we can, again, leave some important decisions up to local government. But providing all of the money (or most of the money) based on a comprehensive national standard tied to local cost-of-living indices would be more efficient and fairer than the system we now have.

Finally, the desire for a fairer society should lead the Democrats to support economic policies which will benefit working-class and poor Americans. The richest Americans gained wealth (even after controlling for inflation) in the 1980s, but most Americans were neither better nor worse off than they had been prior to the Reagan years. As we saw in Chapter 3, and as Robert Kuttner has argued convincingly, policies of economic populism are strong unifying policies for the Democrats. Even conservative Republican analyst Kevin Phillips has noted the increasing division in the United States between rich and poor and its potential for remaking the American political landscape.[2] The Democrats should push hard for policies which lead to fairer economic outcomes for millions of Americans. Kuttner, for example, argues for "an ongoing system of training and job upgrading that also serves to take up slack in the labor market, so that workers don't find themselves involuntarily on the streets."[3]

He also advocates policies which will revitalize labor unions and lead to a new social contract between industry and labor with a constructive, positive role for the latter. For example, he supports a number of initiatives, including reformed labor law, subsidies, management training, and grants for pilot programs, which increase union responsibility for enforcing health and safety regulations. And as he notes, the Democrats need to be "serious and explicit about their public philosophy."[4] They need to make it clear that they want to restructure corporate-labor relations to empower workers and give people greater control over their daily existence. By making government more relevant to people's lives, the Democratic Party can rebuild the public support necessary for progressive policies to succeed.

I am not going to go into detail about the specific policies the Democrats should support. (I leave that task to the policy experts!) Rather, the point is that there are many areas where progressive policy is also good politics. The Democrats need to reaffirm their commitment to such policies and push clearly and explicitly for them. They need to reaffirm their commitment to making American society more just and fair and to making government more relevant to people's everyday lives. As we have seen, there is strong public support for such policies, and they will tend to pull the New Deal coalition (with the exception of upper-class southern whites) together. Reconnecting people with the political world can rebuild a stable progressive Democratic majority.

Paying the Piper: Taxes and the Republican Challenge

Building public connections to government will, of course, take time. The current public mood is skeptical and distrustful of government, and the Democrats will not be able to build these ties overnight. In addition, there are two other problems such an ambitious political agenda will face: the need for revenues, and Republican attempts to drive wedges in the Democratic Party.

Taxes

We looked at public opposition to taxes in Chapter 4. As noted there, public opposition is not to taxes per se but to the perceived unfairness of the tax system. And that is what the Democrats need to focus on. The Democrats need to work for a more progressive and fair tax system. Corporate taxes and taxes on the wealthy should take an increasing proportion of tax revenues. It is important to shift taxes from less progressive state and local taxes to more progressive federal taxes. The smaller the locality, the more power wealthy individuals and corporations have to shape tax policy. If I think property taxes are too high in my community, I can move to the community next door. Such a move involves some but not a lot of cost. Moving across state lines to avoid state taxes is more difficult but still possible. Leaving the country is an even more difficult option. Thus, I can put a great deal of pressure on localities to keep my taxes low, but as I move up the scale, my influence lessens. The threat to relocate "if I don't get a better deal" and the need to "create a climate in which businesses will locate" is weaker at the national level than the state level. Thus, progressive changes in tax laws are more likely at the national than the state level, and at the state level than at the local level. At the state level, then, I would recommend that Democrats push for a transfer of tax revenues from local property taxes to state income taxes. Similarly, the revenue-sharing proposal suggested earlier in this chapter can be tied to a promise to lower state and local taxes to make up for whatever revenue increases are necessary to fund such programs at the national level.

I have no illusions that the programs I recommend above will not cost money and that cuts in defense spending (which the Democrats should push for) will cover the cost. Given the enormous federal deficit and the savings and loan bailout, there will be a need for more revenues. The Democrats need to be clear that the money they raise will go to programs with broad public support. They cannot simply "tax and tax." As Kuttner notes, the derogatory "tax and tax, spend and spend" label pinned on the Democrats by Ronald Reagan actually was first formulated by FDR's aide Harry Hopkins. What Hopkins actually said was, "Tax and tax, spend and spend, elect and elect."[5] If the Democrats are spending money on programs that people support, the public will pay taxes and they will vote for Democrats.

Thus, the Democrats should not be afraid to raise the issue of bringing in more revenues by enhancing the fairness of the tax code. It might also be necessary to institute a value-added tax (national sales tax) along the lines found in most Western European democracies. Clearly, such a tax should include exemptions for basic necessities such as food and clothing (at least under a certain price), in order to prevent it from being regressive. Its rate also could be designed to increase for higher-priced goods, again enhancing progressivity. There are dangers of regressivity in such a tax, but a carefully designed value-added tax could raise revenues to fund the programs needed to revitalize American society. "Selling" such programs to the American public would not be easy. But public attitudes on taxes are not as one-sided as they are often made out to be. The Democrats should stand strongly behind the need to develop and pay for programs to make our society more just and fair and to improve the quality of life for all Americans.

The Republican Challenge

Firmness in this position will also help with the second problem the Democrats face: Republican attempts to discredit the party. This problem has two aspects, the Democrats' image as a party and the ability of the Republicans to exploit that image by focusing on a few policy areas, particularly foreign policy (and patriotism), crime, and, perhaps most importantly, race. As noted in Chapter 2, Democrats in general, and liberals in particular, have an image problem. This problem is connected more to views of the "style" of liberal Democrats than to dissatisfaction with policy proposals. Liberals are seen as being weak, overly concerned with the rights of criminals at the expense of victims, and too willing to help "special interests" (usually minorities, women, and labor). In part, this image problem can be addressed by firmly supporting the kinds of policies I have outlined, which provide benefits for a broad range of citizens. Broad-based social programs in housing, health care, and child care can help counter the view that liberals no longer care about the middle class.

In addition, the Democrats need to stand firm in their views. Shifting with the political winds simply reinforces the impression that the Democrats have no principles. One of Ronald Reagan's strengths as a politician was that one always knew where he stood on the issues. The Democrats need that same kind of consistency. Supporting the abolition of the death penalty, for example, does not have to be a sign of weakness. It can be used as a sign of strength. New York Governor Mario Cuomo, for example, has never been hurt by his opposition to the death penalty. He couples that opposition with a strong commitment to sentences of mandatory life imprisonment without parole and is able, as a result, to maintain an image of strength. Other death penalty opponents need to learn the same lesson. They must make it clear that opposition to the death penalty is not support for criminals and crime. When Michael Dukakis was asked in the 1988 presidential debate if he would still oppose the death penalty if his wife was the victim, Dukakis should have responded by expressing his hope that anyone who committed such a crime would be punished in such a way that he would never be able to do so again but that such a punishment did not mean society had to kill him. Life imprisonment without parole was an alternative. And from there Dukakis could have moved to a discussion of how to deal, realistically, with the problem of crime, pointing out that the death penalty will not solve the crime problem. (A focus on gun control might also have been in order, thereby turning the tables on Republicans who oppose gun control measures supported by a vast majority of the American public.)

This issue of strength is also important in foreign policy discussions. Weakness on defense issues is another part of the liberal Democratic image. But again, there is a positive side that can be drawn on. As we have seen, the American public is not supportive of increasing defense spending. The public sees both education and economic development as more important for our long-term security interests in a changing world than developing new weapons. Progressive Democrats need to make that argument clearly. Strength through a better economy and technological leadership is one important theme that liberal Democrats need to stress. In addition, progressive Democrats need to make it clear that they do support maintaining our military strength. We may not need to build every weapons system the Pentagon desires, and we may not need as many weapons as conservative Republicans argue for, but as the crisis in the Persian Gulf illustrates, there is still a need for military forces.

The Persian Gulf crisis has other lessons as well. Our dependence on foreign oil, an important issue in the 1970s which was ignored by the Reagan-Bush Administration, has once again come into focus. So have the consequences of befriending dictators such as Saddam Hussein, who was "on our side" when he fought against Iran. Liberal Democrats should point out the need for a foreign policy based on support for human rights and freedom abroad (principles which, as we have seen, have strong public backing), and the dangers of dealing with dictators and despots who seem to offer short-term political advantage. George Bush has spent much of his time in foreign policy undoing the ill effects of our alliances with Manuel Noriega and Saddam Hussein during the Reagan years. The war against Saddam Hussein was, in most minds, a stunning success. But a successful war that is needed to clean up the mistakes of previous foreign policy alliances should not be seen as proof of the effectiveness of the Bush Administration's foreign policy. A more progressive, enlightened foreign policy might have avoided a war in the Persian Gulf. Liberal Democrats should not be afraid to make that case clearly and consistently. Such an approach will, certainly, lead to charges that the Democrats are soft on defense. But backtracking, obfuscating, or riding in tanks will not solve the problem. They will only make the Democrats look defensive and unsure of themselves. A clear, consistent view of what national security entails and what our foreign policy goals should be is the best way to deal with these image problems.

Similarly, the Democrats do not need to tie themselves up in knots over issues of "patriotism." The Pledge of Allegiance issue or the question of burning the American flag should not concern progressive Democrats. Being forthright should. A strong, clear statement supporting the right of people to burn the American flag or to refuse to say the Pledge of Allegiance, no matter how abhorrent we find such action, is the key factor. Progressive Democrats need to make it clear that their position on these issues reflects their patriotism and belief in the principles for which America stands. Legalistic defenses based on constitutionality are misplaced. Strong support of principle is what is needed. Furthermore, progressives should not be afraid to throw these issues back to the Republicans. Ask those who want to ban the burning of the American flag if they support the right of Chinese authorities to jail a citizen who burns the Chinese flag as a symbol of protest. Ask why we should deny rights to American citizens which we would applaud should they be granted in other countries. These issues are not of major importance to most Americans. People do not vote based on where candidates stand on these issues, so long as that stand is not seen as a sign of weakness or disrespect for America. Once these issues are made more complicated and begin to cut both ways, my guess is that they will disappear rapidly from the political scene.

Finally, there is the issue of race. As noted in Chapter 3, the Democrats do have the image of being "too concerned" with minorities. On the other hand, public support for civil rights and racial equality is also clear. The Democrats need to emphasis the strength of their commitment to a more egalitarian society. The thorny issue is affirmative action and "quotas." As we have seen, most Americans (including a majority of African-Americans) oppose affirmative action programs because they do not think it is "fair" to give special privileges to minorities (or women) over "better qualified" white males. And this is a particularly potent issue among working-class whites, who are part of the Democrats' natural constituency. These people often feel affirmative action programs are unfair to them. Thus, this issue is very divisive for the Democrats.

I would be lying if I said this will be an easy issue for progressive Democrats to deal with. Even when affirmative action programs do not entail quotas, it is easy to make the argument that they do, and Republicans, conservatives, and other opponents of affirmative action will be sure to make that case (as the battle over the Civil Rights Act of 1990 showed). I do not think, however, that the Democrats should back away from their commitment to such programs. But they do need to recognize their problem. There are two things that liberal Democrats should do to lessen its divisiveness. First, they must continue to stress a commitment to a just society. There is no place for racial prejudice in American society, and the Democrats should draw on their heritage in that regard. They should not turn their backs on affirmative action programs simply because they are unpopular. They need to point to the continuing need for such programs in contemporary America. Working to convince white Americans of the racial barriers that still exist today can help. The large gap in perceptions about these barriers cited in Chapter 6 makes it clear that this will not be an easy task, but standing up for principles of justice and racial equality is important.

Second, the party must stress the fact that a major part of the problem facing African-Americans in today's society results from the "politics of rich and poor," since a disproportionate percentage of minority citizens are poor. Thus, many of the solutions are the same programs which will help working-class white Americans. The problems of health care, housing, child care, and economic opportunity are problems which cut across racial lines, and instituting programs to help solve these problems will greatly enhance the opportunities for African-American citizens as well as for poor and working class white Americans. Progressive Democrats need to focus on the problems which unite their coalition. If there is to be a battle between "us" and "them," Democrats need working-class and middle-class white Americans to shift their thinking so that "them" becomes not "blacks" but "the rich."

Two final points about the policy stands that liberal Democrats should take to build a winning coalition. First, as I have frequently argued, many progressive policies have broad public support. The public unhappiness with liberal Democrats stems from other sources. Thus, with only a few exceptions, simply supporting liberal and progressive policy positions is good politics. I have discussed some of these positions above, but that list is not exhaustive. For example, support for women's rights and feminism is similar to support for civil rights. With the exception of affirmative action, the public offers broad support for securing more equal opportunities for women (even if it does not like the term "feminism").[6] Thus, progressive Democrats should not be afraid to support a wide range of progressive policies.

And second, the Democrats should not hesitate to raise issues which will tend to divide the Republican coalition. For some reason that I have never been able to understand, the Republican Party has always made better use of issues such as the death penalty, affirmative action, and a strong national defense than the Democrats have made of the issues which can put Republicans on the defensive. Since the *Webster* decision, the Democrats have gotten better at using the abortion issue to their political advantage. But Democrats also need to push policies in areas such as the environment, gun control, and education where the Republican position clearly runs counter to an almost united public.

Conclusion

Progressive politics, then, are good politics. They enjoy widespread popular support, but only if the Democrats can overcome the strong distrust of government in any form that is so prevalent in American society. A series of policies which rebuilds the ties that citizens have with their government is the solution to this problem. Relying on local government to make decisions puts authority at a level where people are more likely to feel connected and to have influence. Instituting policies which help people with the problems they face in their lives (such as housing and health care) can rebuild the ties people feel with government.

The goal of a progressive Democratic administration should be to reassert the value of the use of government as a tool of our collective conscience. Government can help us achieve the kind of society we want. It can help create a community. We need to recognize government as a tool of the people, not the enemy. But that will only happen if people feel connected to and a part of their government. If we centralize financing, raising more of our revenues at the national level, but decentralize, as much as possible, the decisions about how money should be spent, we will maximize the potential for allowing that connection to grow.

But creating policies which can increase these ties and pushing for progressive policies is only part of the battle. If the Democrats are to rebuild a progressive governing coalition, they also need to rebuild their party. In the final chapter, we will turn to party building and the issue of money in contemporary American politics.

9

Rebuilding the
Democratic Party:
Politics from the Bottom Up

In order to rebuild a progressive governing coalition, the Democratic Party needs to strengthen itself as a party. Not only do Democrats need to connect people with government; they also need to connect people with the party. As Walter Dean Burnham has written:

> To state the matter with utmost simplicity: political parties, with all their well-known human and structural shortcomings, are the only devices thus far invented by the wit of Western man which with some effectiveness can generate countervailing collective power on behalf of the many powerless against the relatively few who are individually—or organizationally—powerful.[1]

The Democratic Party must revitalize itself in order to play that role. A stronger, more active party can organize lower-, working-, and middle-class Americans in support of the kinds of policies outlined in Chapter 8. But just as rebuilding support for active government will take time, so will building active support for the Democratic Party.

Making Party Relevant

The American public has always had ambivalent attitudes toward political parties.[2] We recognize their importance, but we do not trust them. Thus, for example, close to two-thirds of the public believes that parties do make a difference. On the other hand, we are taught in school to "vote for the person, not for the party." In a survey measuring citizen attitudes toward parties, Larry Sabato found that 92 percent of the public agreed with this sentiment.[3]

It is particularly important for the Democrats to revitalize public support for parties. Politics without parties or with weak parties does not have an equal effect on the Democrats and the Republicans. Weaker parties means a stronger influence for those with the individual and collective resources to be involved in the political system, and that means more power for the wealthy and for interest groups. As E.E. Schattschneider noted, "The flaw in the pluralist heaven is that the heavenly choir sings with a strong upper-class accent."[4] Stronger parties are more important to Democratic constituencies than to Republican constituencies. There are a number of things the Democrats can do to help increase the strength of political parties in general and themselves in particular.

Building Strong Local Parties

First, the Democrats need to concentrate on building strong grassroots parties. The best way to revitalize parties is to involve people with them. Getting the party involved in the local issues that matter in people's day-to-day lives is important. Thus, the policy goal of leaving important decisions to local government should be coupled with an attempt to build local party organizations to influence those decisions. Increasing the power of the people should be both a policy goal and a party goal. And when local governments have decisions to make that will influence important aspects of people's lives, it will be easier to convince people to get involved.

Local parties should, therefore, become active even in areas which are often seen as "nonpartisan," such as school board elections. Local Democratic parties should support candidates in school board elections and work for better schools. Such actions will, inevitably, bring charges of "politicizing" education. The party, however, should remain firm in its view that working to see that the best people get elected to school boards will help improve the community and reaffirm the goal of the party to make communities better places to live.

The party should also be active in other matters of local concern such as environmental issues (recycling, solid waste disposal, clean air and water, parks and recreation), fire and police protection, and fair and equitable economic growth. Strong and active local parties can make a difference in people's lives, and the Democratic Party should work to make that difference.

Similarly, Larry Sabato suggests that political parties set up mobile offices with "ombudsmen" to help people deal with government and the bureaucracy. As he notes, people in the United States rarely look to parties to help them with the problems they face with government, but 58 percent of the public agreed that it would be a good idea for parties to become more active as social and civic organizations which helped people deal with government. (The percentage of blacks, women, and Democrats who supported this proposition was even higher.) Such activities would give the party a chance to play a positive role in people's lives. Members of Congress might not like the competition they would face as they now have a virtual monopoly on such service, but the long term interests of the parties in general, and the Democrats in particular, would be well served by such activities.[5]

Harry Boyte's book *CommonWealth* looks at the possibilities of citizen involvement in the political process. He argues that the tradition of citizen politics in the United States is alive and well, and that when it is working, it creates "the sense of politics as an ongoing activity among equals." He points to a number of well-organized local citizen organizations which have had success and how such organizations serve as both means and ends. They are means to achieving more progressive policy goals, but they are ends in themselves, for the very process of bringing people into the political system creates a more democratic society.[6] The ex-

amples he cites are of independent local groups not tied to the
existing political structure. But there is no reason that a revitalized Democratic Party cannot play the role he outlines for local
citizen organizations. In fact, because it can link local organizations into a broader national coalition, the possibility for long-
term success in implementing progressive political policies
would be enhanced by such an arrangement. Local Democratic
Party organizations need to see themselves as active, vital
links between citizens and government. They need to help increase the involvement of people in their communities. And
they need to fight for changes which will empower people to
make decisions about their own lives and the lives of their
communities.

Revitalizing the Election Process

A second set of party building activities involves the American
electoral process. There are a number of changes the Democrats
should work for to create a political environment which will
connect people with government and rebuild political parties.
Part of this has to do with the issue of money, which we will look
at shortly, but there are several other changes the Democrats
should work for in the way we elect our political leaders.

First, the Democrats should favor eliminating "nonpartisan"
local elections. Identifying candidates by party on electoral bal-
lots is advantageous to the Democrats. In nonpartisan elections,
money becomes more important (as candidates need to do more
to let people know who they are). Better-educated, wealthier citizens become more important. Organized interest groups (especially business interests) become more important. And thus,
"Republican" interests are better served in a "nonpartisan" environment than are "Democratic" interests. If candidates are identified
by party, even citizens who pay little attention to politics will have
something to go on in the voting booth. If they are not so identified,
the candidate with better connections to funding sources and, therefore, the larger advertising budget, is even more advantaged.

Partisan local elections will make the revitalization of local party organizations easier. Even in the absence of partisan elections, local Democratic parties should run candidates for office. But that task is easier if the ballot sanctions such activities.

Secondly, the Democrats should work to increase the number of states which use or allow conventions or caucuses for nominating candidates and to limit the use of primaries. (At a minimum, they should work for preprimary conventions to endorse candidates officially.) The major advantage of conventions and caucuses is that they help rebuild party organizations. Those citizens willing to come to caucuses and conventions make up an automatic list of party volunteers and workers. The very act of getting involved in these activities brings people closer to the party. Unlike primaries, where voters go into a booth and make a choice and are never heard from again, caucuses and conventions create a situation where Democrats meet each other and can learn to work together. In addition, caucuses and conventions are less expensive for candidates than primaries, and anything that reduces the costs of the electoral process is helpful to progressive Democrats.

There are those who will argue that primaries are "more democratic." But the advantages in that direction are more apparent than real. First, the United States is the only democracy in the world where parties do not have control over their own nominations. Returning this power to the parties will not preclude "democracy." I am not advocating a return to selections of nominees in "smoke-filled rooms" outside the view of the public. But a system of open caucuses or conventions where participation is open to all who think of themselves as "Democrats" can retain the advantages of public participation while also better serving the purpose of party building. Second, turnout in primaries is even lower than in general elections. A system which relies on the personal popularity of the candidates among primary voters will not necessarily pick the "most democratically popular" candidate among general election voters. Allowing a group of interested citizens to meet and discuss the best options for a candidate may, in fact, lead to better nominees. It is true that turnout will be even lower than in primaries, but the nature of such meetings means that those selecting the nominees will be forced to spend more time thinking about how others will view the candidate and less on their personal feelings than is the case in a primary election. Which system, in the end, is "more democratic" may not be as clear as proponents of primaries argue. And third, having candidates run primary campaigns where they attack their fellow partisans does not benefit either party in the long run. Better to save one's campaigning for the general election.

The Democrats should also work for the provision of free television and radio time *for the parties* during elections. The cost of campaigning has grown enormously, and public dissatisfaction with the vast amounts of money spent in campaigns is one of the reasons the public is so alienated from the election process. Free media time for parties can help get spending down (and reduce the financial disadvantage faced by many progressive Democratic candidates). It also has practical advantages over providing free time directly to candidates. Giving free media time to congressional candidates in major metropolitan areas is a logistical nightmare. Each media market includes too many different districts to make such arrangements feasible. Providing such time to the parties, however, to dole out to candidates (or use for generic party advertising) eliminates such problems and strengthens the parties at the same time.

The most important change, however, that is needed in the electoral process is an increase in voter turnout. The United States has, with the possible exception of Switzerland, the lowest voter turnout among all western democracies. And, as we have seen in Chapter 6, turnout is very skewed by class. Republican segments of the population turn out in much higher numbers than Democratic segments. Part of the turnout problem is the growing alienation from the political system which I have discussed. And policies and programs which reconnect the public with the political system will likely increase turnout. If people see that politics matters, they are more likely to vote.

Similarly, lessening the influence of money in campaigns

(which we will turn to shortly) will also make people feel as if their participation matters. When the public sees millions of dollars being spent by candidates for the United States Senate, it often concludes that no matter who wins, those who paid will be those with influence. It does not matter whether or not one can "buy" an election or a member of Congress (a topic which political scientists often debate),[7] what matters is the perception that one can. When the costs of elections are as high as they are, citizens with little or no financial resources are bound to feel as if their efforts matter less to candidates than those with the money to help in campaigns. Scandals such as the "Keating Five" simply reinforce that perception. The defense used by those charged with taking money in return for helping Charles Keating—that there was no quid pro quo and that they were simply trying to help a constituent—even if true, simply further erodes confidence in the system. Most people know that their U.S. Senator would not make that kind of effort on their behalf even if they had contributed $25 to his or her campaign.

Lowering the barriers to voting can also improve voting turnout. As Piven and Cloward document, voter registration laws tend to have a stronger impact on citizens less firmly connected to the electoral system. Easing those requirements would help to increase turnout. More importantly, in combination with policies and party activities which reconnect citizens with the political system, easing registration requirements would help to lessen the class bias in voting and the Republican turnout advantage. As Piven and Cloward note, the relationship between turnout and class and registration laws is not a simple, direct one. Stricter registration laws do not automatically lead to a class bias in voting, but they do create the conditions which make such a bias more likely. Easing registration requirements will not automatically close the gap in turnout between rich and poor, but it will create the circumstances which make it easier to close that gap.[8]

Changes in voter registration laws will not be easy to attain. Elected officials have all been victorious under the current set of rules, and thus even many Democratic officials are reluctant to change the rules and create uncertainties in the electoral process.[9] On the other hand, it is clearly in the long-run interests of progressive Democrats to increase the party's base of voters among poor white and minority voters. These voters currently have a low turnout rate, but when they do vote, they vote substantially more Democratic (and support progressive economic policies) than other segments of the electorate. The Democrats, consequently, should push for postcard registration or programs which allow easy or automatic registration by government agencies (such as the "motor voter" plans which allow registration at motor vehicle bureaus), or, best of all, election-day registration. Similarly, the party should push for making election day a holiday (or moving it to Sunday), so that working-class voters can more easily get to the polls.

Finally, voter registration drives and get-out-the-vote drives should be a regular part of the Democratic Party's activities. It is not enough to work to make it easier to vote. The Democrats should work to get people to vote. Again, the best incentive to vote is a sense that politics matters, so that pursuing party and policy goals which connect people with the political system is, in a sense, the best kind of "get-out-the-vote drive." But traditional grass-roots, door knocking, voter registration and get-out-the-vote drives still have a role to play.

The problem that is left, however, is that all of these party-building activities, as well as campaigns in general, cost money. And the need to raise money can push the Democrats away from a progressive platform and more toward "the center." We need then, finally, to turn to the issue of money and the American electoral process.

Money and American Elections

The need to raise money creates major problems for the Democratic Party. For the Republicans, money and ideology flow together. Raising money from corporate political action committees and wealthy individuals fits nicely with a political platform which protects the interests of those groups. For Democrats, on the other hand, money and ideology diverge. Raising money from political action committees and wealthy individuals takes the party away from its base of support among working- and lower-class citizens. Money puts cross-pressures on Democratic candidates and officeholders.[10] There are three solutions to this dilemma that the Democrats need to pursue.

First, in the long-run, the Democrats need to work for a system of public campaign financing. Public financing of elections would cut the ties between money and the election process. Of course, that does not mean that the wealthy and corporate interests would lose all influence. Money has many ways of making itself felt. And reducing its use in campaigns will not eliminate its use as a political tool. On the other hand, freeing candidates from money in the electoral process strengthens the role of ordinary voters in that process, and, perhaps just as importantly, can help to reestablish public faith in the fairness of the process. If full public funding is not possible (because of cost or political opposition), the Democrats should work for changes which encourage small individual contributions, perhaps through tax incentives for such contributions, or limited matching funds.

It also would be helpful to tie any public-funding mechanisms to the parties rather than to individual candidates. Similarly, encouraging individuals (through tax incentives or differences in limits) to donate money to parties rather than individual candidates should be pursued. As noted above, in the long run, strengthening the parties as institutions can only help progressive politics. Shifting the focus of campaign finance away from individual candidates and toward the parties will help in that regard. In the short run, the greater financial resources of the Republican Party and the ability of Democratic incumbents to raise money as individuals to overcome those party differences, may make such a policy seem counterproductive. But in the long-run, progressive politics benefits from cutting the importance of money and increasing the role of political parties in the electoral process.

Second, as noted above, Democrats should work to lessen the

importance of money in political campaigns by supporting mandated free television and radio time to the political parties. The public should reassert its right to control the public airwaves and tell the large corporations which operate very profitable television and radio stations that in return for access to those airwaves they must enable the public to have fair election campaigns on television and radio. Similarly, free mailings of campaign literature should be mandated as well.

Finally, if no public funding is implemented or until it is, the Democrats need to divorce themselves from political action committee money and build a reliable list of small contributors to fund political campaigns and party activities of the kind described above. Kuttner notes some of the relatively successful efforts that Democrats have undertaken in that regard. Building up a larger base in this area is essential.[11]

It is true that even these individual contributors will be wealthier than the average Democratic voter. On the other hand, small individual contributions from middle-class Democrats do not have the same kind of institutional pull as larger corporate and individual contributions. Furthermore, the most successful fundraising efforts targeted at individuals are those that rely on explicitly ideological appeals.[12] Thus, unlike soliciting money from corporate political action committees, soliciting money from small contributions in direct mail campaigns will cause the party to emphasize the most progressive aspects of its platform. Raising money is always likely to be more of a problem for the Democrats than the Republicans. Republicans are richer. But at least reliance on direct-mail campaigns and small contributions will push the Democrats into a more coherent progressive ideological appeal.

I think it is important to note two additional points concerning money. The first is that we often overemphasize the importance of money in today's campaign environment. The second is that the issue of money is also a potential progressive political issue which the Democrats should exploit.

There is no doubt that money is an important political

resource. As Gary Jacobson has shown quite convincingly, underfunded challengers rarely stand a chance against Congressional incumbents.[13] On the other hand, once challengers reach a certain level of funding, money is much less important, I would argue, than we often think it is. Thus, for example, of the six senatorial challengers who beat incumbents in 1986, four— Brock Adams of Washington, Kent Conrad of North Dakota, Wyche Fowler of Georgia, and Richard Shelby of Alabama— were substantially outspent by their incumbent opponents, while the other two—Bob Graham of Florida and Tom Daschle of South Dakota—spent essentially the same amount of money as their incumbent opponents. (The three winning senatorial challengers in 1988 all spent approximately the same amount of money as their incumbent opponents.) Similarly, the one victorious senatorial challenger in 1990, Paul Wellstone of Minnesota, was outspent by $6.4 million to $780,000! And Anne Richards was elected as Governor of Texas despite her opponent Clayton Williams's $20 million campaign expenditures, while Lawton Chiles was elected Governor of Florida although he was outspent two-to-one by incumbent Bob Martinez and refused to accept contributions of over $100.[14]

The point is not that money is not important. It is. Consider that in 1990, according to Common Cause, of the 124 House incumbents who had faced challengers with more than $25,000 but less than half the money the incumbent had, only 6 were defeated. Of the 35 incumbents who faced challengers who raised more than half the money the incumbent had, 9 were able to win.[15]

On the other hand, money is clearly not everything, and the Democrats, especially progressive Democrats, would do well to focus more of their energies on traditional grass-roots style campaigning. Such campaigning not only can help overcome financial disparities, it also can bring the kinds of connections to politics that media campaigns cannot. Raising money is important. But it should not become so much of a focus of the campaigns of progressive Democrats that old-style, people-oriented grass-roots campaigning is ignored.

Furthermore, the question of money in campaigns is another issue that progressive Democrats can use to their advantage. Refusing contributions from political action committees and attacking Republicans for being beholden to special interests can have widespread appeal, particularly if coupled with a refusal to accept large individual contributions. Lawton Chiles's gubernatorial election in Florida in 1990 was conducted, in part, around such a theme. Drawing attention to the Democrat's connections with middle- and working-class Americans by refusing "big money" can help reinforce a positive image of Democrats for people. Paul Wellstone in Minnesota in 1990 made great use of the fact that Rudy Boschwitz had a lot more money than he did. The public does not like the influence of money in the political process. And while, unfortunately, it still takes money to get a message across (even one about the lack of money), a progressive political campaign should include both the goal of weakening the influence of money and as little reliance on "big money" as is possible. Sticking to such an appeal can strengthen the public's perception of the Democrats as the party of "the common person," and help to overcome the alienation and distance that so many Americans feel from the political process.

Conclusion

The goal of the Democratic Party, then, must be to reconnect people and politics. The party needs to work to make government a positive force which improves the lives of Americans and our communities. Democrats should advocate policies which use the collective power of government to help ordinary citizens in areas such as health care, education, and child care. They should advocate economic programs which work to the benefit of working- and lower-class Americans by providing jobs, opportunities and resources. And they should advocate policies which empower the public by giving people more access over the decisions which government makes and, consequently, more power over their own lives.

The argument of this book has been that such policies are also good politics. The way for the Democrats to regain power and the Presidency on a long-term basis is to move in a progressive, or liberal, direction. There is public support for most of the progressive agenda, and the New Deal coalition, while weakened, is still largely intact. Building on it by appealing to traditional Democratic constituencies with progressive economic, social, and foreign policies is the best hope for the Democratic Party. It is true that such appeals will create some tensions within the Democratic coalition. But as we have seen, a progressive appeal creates more cohesion and unity than is sometimes believed. Furthermore, such an appeal will have the geographic popularity to win enough votes in the electoral college to capture the Presidency.

This is not to say there are not barriers to building a progressive coalition. The three most important are public dissatisfaction with paying taxes, public distrust of government, and race. But as I have tried to show, the public's aversion to taxes seems to have more to do with the fairness of the system than with the level of taxes, and the Democrats should not be afraid to propose changes in the tax code. In fact, restructuring the tax system both to make it fairer and to pay for programs which the public wants should be central to any progressive appeal. Furthermore, I have argued, good progressive politics would push for policies which can, in the long run, reconnect people with the political system and lessen the alienation that now exists. Democrats can also undertake a number of initiatives to rebuild the party at the grass-roots level as another way of reconnecting people to the political world. Finally, with regards to race, the Democrats need to shift the perceptions of middle- and working-class white Americans so that "us and them" becomes not "white and black," but "rich and poor." This will not, of course, be easy. But a commitment to those same kinds of policies which rebuild people's connections with government, and convince people that government is working to make our society a more just, fair, and equitable one, can also help to shift Americans away from the politics of race.

The increasing gap between rich and poor and the increasing dissatisfaction that people feel with the political system present an opportunity for progressives and liberals to redefine the political landscape away from the conservatism and materialism of the Reagan years and toward a more equitable, just vision of the social world. The public never accepted the Reagan agenda. If progressive Democrats recognize that and use the raw materials available to build a party dedicated to a very different vision of our collective life, then the party can once more play a central role in defining our political agenda and our political culture. If they continue to vacillate back and forth, or if they accept the Republican notions of a conservative public and limited government, then the public will continue to reward them with electoral defeat.

Alternatively, if the Democrats happen to win an election because the public is dissatisfied with Republican policies without outlining a clear, coherent, distinctive public philosophy, then that victory will be hollow. Without a clear progressive agenda, a Democrat would find him or herself in the White House without the support necessary to revitalize government and to begin to solve the problems facing the United States as we head into the twenty-first century. In today's media-dominated political environment, public support of major policy changes is crucial. Without a clearly defined vision and without a new level of public trust and confidence, resistance to progressive policies will remain strong. If the public is going to turn to the Democrats to govern, the Democrats need to offer them a choice. Accepting the Republican definition of what is or is not possible in our current political context is tantamount to defeat. The public can be receptive to a broader vision of what is possible. If the Democrats remember that and appeal to that vision, they can win. More importantly, if they do win, they can begin to implement a political program which can reconnect people with government and build a more lasting progressive governing coalition. The Democratic Party needs to get back to its progressive tradition in order to make that vision possible. Progressive politics is good politics. That is the lesson the Democrats need to learn.

Notes

Chapter 2

1. Both quotations are cited in Robin Toner, "Dukakis Aides Acknowledge Bush Outmaneuvered Them," pp. A1, A8.

2. See James Ceaser, "The Reagan Presidency and American Public Opinion," pp. 172–210.

3. Steven Weisman, "Can the Magic Prevail?" p.39.

4. Charles Ostrom, Jr., and Dennis Simon,"The Man in the Teflon Suit?" p. 383.

5. See, for example, Ceaser, "The Reagan Presidency and American Public Opinion"; Thomas Ferguson and Joel Rogers, *Right Turn: The 1984 Election and the Future of American Politics*; Arthur Sanders and Kenneth Wagner, "The Myth of Charisma in American Politics"; Lee Sigelman and Kathleen Knight, "Expectation/Disillusion and Presidential Popularity: The Reagan Experience"; and William Adams, "Recent Fables about Ronald Reagan."

6. The *New York Times* data are cited on July 11, 1987, p. A1. The Gallup data are from *The Gallup Report*, May 1989, p. 23.

7. See Dan Nimmo and James Coombs, *Mediated Political Realities*.

8. See Murray Edelman, *Constructing the Political Spectacle*, and *The Symbolic Uses of Politics*.

9. See Edward Epstein, *News from Nowhere*, and Austin Ranney, *Channels of Power*.

10. For a good summary see Doris Graber, *Mass Media and American Politics*, or Sidney Kraus and Dennis Davis, *The Effects of Mass Communication on Political Behavior*.

11. While these in-depth interviews are not any kind of a random sample (no sample of twenty-six individuals is large enough to allow concrete generalizations to the broader public), they were extremely illuminating in helping to understand how people seem to sort through the political world. The lack of

generalizability was more than compensated for by the depth of understanding. See Arthur Sanders, *Making Sense of Politics*.

12. See Benjamin Page, *Choices and Echoes in Presidential Elections*, especially Chapter 8; Sanders, *Making Sense of Politics*; or Jeffrey Smith, *American Presidential Elections: Trust and the Rational Voter*.

13. See Sanders, *Making Sense of Politics*, especially Chapter 8. In that chapter, I show evidence from the 1984 American National Election Study that indicates that among the general population, stylistic voters are much more influenced by retrospective evaluations than are policy voters. For similar findings from the 1988 American National Election Study, see Arthur Sanders, "Making Sense of Politics," a paper presented at the annual meeting of the American Political Science Association, Washington, DC, 1991.

14. The most comprehensive discussion of these matters is Morris Fiorina, *Retrospective Voting in American National Elections*.

15. Ceasar, "The Reagan Presidency and American Public Opinion," p. 204.

16. The data from the American National Election Study Series cited in this book were all made available through the Interuniversity Consortium for Political and Social Research. Neither the consortium nor the original investigators for any of the studies bear any responsibility for the interpretations presented here.

17. See the *Washington Post*, October 23, 1991, pp. A1, A11.

18. Jean Bethke Elshtain, "Issues and Themes in the 1988 Campaign."

19. One of the most striking things I found in my in-depth interviews was how often people raised issues of trust, and how central these attitudes seemed to be to their thinking about politics. See Chapter 3 of *Making Sense of Politics*.

Chapter 3

1. Unless otherwise noted, the data in this chapter are from the 1988 American National Election Study. The 23 percent liberal represents the total of those saying they were "extremely liberal" (2 percent), "liberal" (8), and "slightly liberal" (13).

2. See Pamela Conover and Stanley Feldman, "The Origins and Meaning of Liberal/Conservative Self-Identifications"; Henry Brady and Paul Sniderman, "Attitude Attribution: A Group Basis for Political Reasoning"; Kathleen Knight, "Ideological Identification and the Content of the Ideological Agenda, 1960–1980"; and Arthur Sanders, "The Meaning of Liberalism and Conservatism."

3. For a fuller explication see Arthur Sanders, "Ideological Symbols."

4. See Sanders,"The Meaning of Liberalism and Conservatism."

5. Lloyd Free and Hadley Cantril, *The Political Beliefs of Americans*.

6. Celinda Lake and Stanley Greenberg, "What's Left for Liberalism."

7. See Thomas Ferguson and Joel Rogers, *Right Turn: The 1984 Election and the Future of American Politics*.

8. Ibid., p. 14.

9. Jerry Yeric and John Todd, *Public Opinion: The Visible Politics*, p. 192.

10. Lake and Greenberg, "What's Left for Liberalism," p. 7.

11. Ibid.

12. *The Gallup Report*, May 1988, p. 34.

13. Lake and Greenberg, "What's Left for Liberalism," p. 7.

14. John Doble and Keith Melvile, "The Public's Social Welfare Mandate," p. 49.

15. See Arthur Sanders, "Rationality, Self-Interest, and Public Attitudes on Public Spending."

16. See Arthur Sanders, *Making Sense of Politics*, especially pp. 101 and 120–122.

17. Doble and Melville, "The Public's Social Welfare Mandate."

18. Lake and Greenberg, "What's Left for Liberalism," p. 7.

19. *The Gallup Report*, June 1989, pp. 7–9.

20. *The Gallup Report*, July 1988, p. 12, and *The Gallup Poll Monthly*, April, 1991, p. 7.

21. All of these figures come from *The Gallup Report*, July 1986, pp. 17–18.

22. *The Gallup Report*, June 1989, p. 25.

23. *The Gallup Poll Monthly*, January 1990, p. 4.

24. *The Gallup Report*, September 1989, p. 8.

25. *The Gallup Report*, March/April, 1989, pp. 3–4.

26. *The Gallup Report*, August 1988, p. 4.

27. Yeric and Todd, *Public Opinion*, p. 156.

28. Barbara Farah and Ethel Klein, "Public Opinion Trends," p. 117.

29. *The Gallup Report*, October 1989, p. 18.

30. *The Gallup Poll Monthly*, December 1989, p. 15.

31. Linda DeStafano and Diane Colasanto, "Unlike 1975, Today Most Americans Think Men Have It Better."

32. *The Gallup Report*, July 1988, p. 17, DeStafano and Colasanto, "Unlike 1975, Today Most Americans Think Men Have It Better"; and the 1988 American National Election Study. The data from the American National Election Study combines the "1", "2," and "3" responses together for 69 percent supporting the liberal side of the issue, with a full 43 percent at the extreme "1" position. The 14 percent on the conservative side include 6 percent at the extreme "7" position. Seventeen percent of the public placed themselves in the middle "4" position.

33. *The Gallup Poll Monthly*, December 1989, p. 15.

34. *The Gallup Report*, September 1988, p. 46.

35. *The Gallup Report*, October 1989, p. 12.

36. *The Gallup Report*, August 1988, pp. 6–9.

37. Linda Greenhouse, "Despite Support, A Child Care Bill Fails to Emerge," p. A14.

38. Tamar Lewin, "Daycare Becomes a Growing Burden," p. A22.

39. *The Gallup Report*, July 1988, p. 6; and September 1988, pp. 51–52.

40. William Schneider, "Abortion: Trouble for the GOP," and Everett Carl Ladd, "Abortion: Trouble for Both Parties."

41. *The Gallup Report*, July 1989, p. 8.

42. Ibid.

43. Farah and Klein, "Public Opinion Trends," p. 114.

44. Ibid.

45. See Jean Bethke Elshtain, "Issues and Themes in the 1988 Campaign."

46. Farah and Klein, "Public Opinion Trends," p. 114.

47. *The Gallup Poll Monthly*, January 1990, p.10.

48. *The Gallup Report*, July 1988, p. 10.

49. *The Gallup Report*, March 1986, p. 27, and November 1987, p. 6.

50. *The Gallup Report*, May 1986, p. 21.

51. Robin Toner, "Poll Finds Postwar Glow Dimmed by the Economy," p. A11.

52. For information on the change of policy over the banning of chemical weapons, see "Bush Backtracks on Timing of Ban," *Congressional Quarterly Weekly Report*, October 14, 1989, p. 2732. For information on the Bush Administration's opposition to sanctions against Iraq, see "Presidential Opposition to Sanctions Against Iraq for Using Chemical Weapons," *Congressional Quarterly Weekly Report*, September 24, 1988, p. 2634; "Differences on Iraqi Sanctions Complicate Foreign Aid Bill," *Congressional Quarterly Weekly Report*, October 1, 1988, p. 2741; "Senate Panel Seeks Sanctions on Nerve Gas Producers," *Congressional Quarterly Weekly Report*, October 14, 1989, p. 2731; and "Bush's Sanctions Veto Snubs Foreign Relations Leaders," *Congressional Quarterly Weekly Report*, November 24, 1990, p. 3932. The President exercised his veto by refusing to take action on a bill while Congress was adjourned (a "pocket veto"). Given the overwhelming support for the bill in both Houses of Congress, an explicit veto would probably have been overridden.

53. Toner, "Poll Finds Postwar Glow Dimmed by the Economy."

54. *The Gallup Poll Monthly*, February 1990, p. 3.

55. *The Gallup Report*, March 1988, p. 13.

56. For the 1980 election, see Paul Abramson, John Aldrich, and David Rohde, *Change and Continuity in the 1980 Elections;* William Schneider, "The November 4 Vote for President: What Did It Mean?" and Kathleen Frankovic, "Public Opinion Trends." For the 1984 election see Paul Abramson, John Aldrich, and David Rohde, *Change and Continuity in the 1984 Elections;* Scott Keeter, "Public Opinion in 1984," and Theodore Lowi, "An Aligning Election: A Presidential Plebiscite."

Chapter 4

1. Andrew Kohut and Larry Hugick, "Taxes and Federal Programs: Public Supports Higher Taxes for Domestic Programs: Education, Drug War Lead

The List," pp. 4–10. When asked if they were willing to pay $200 per year in taxes, support dropped only slightly. The figures for the four most popular programs with $200 in taxes were Education, 54 percent; Drugs, 52 percent; The Homeless, 46 percent; and Health Care, 48 percent. For similar results see *Public Opinion*, March/April 1989, p. 25.

2. These results are from an AP/Media General survey in November 1988 reported in *Public Opinion*, March/April 1989, p. 26.

3. *The Gallup Report*, July 1988, p. 14.

4. These data are from a survey for the Times Mirror conducted by the Gallup Corporation in May 1988 and were reported in *Public Opinion*, March/April 1989, p. 21.

5. See Arthur Sanders, "Rationality, Self-Interest, and Public Attitudes on Public Spending."

6. *Public Opinion*, March/April 1989, p. 22.

7. *Public Opinion*, March/April 1987, p. 5.

8. Frank Newport, "Tax Reform Fails to Achieve its Goals."

9. See Arthur Sanders, *Making Sense of Politics*, especially the discussion of fairness on pages 119–124.

10. From the Gallup Poll, cited in *Public Opinion*, March/April 1989, p. 23. When Social Security taxes were added to the list in 1988, the figures were: federal income tax: 26 percent; local property tax: 24 percent; social security tax: 17 percent; state sales tax: 15 percent; and state income tax: 9 percent.

11. For a comprehensive discussion of the California "tax revolt," see David Sears and Jack Citrin, *Tax Revolt*.

12. The *Washington Post*, November 9, 1978, p. A5. See also the *New York Times*, January 7, 1987, section 12, p. 12, for a summary of 1978 tax and spending propositions.

13. For information on 1979 tax and spending propositions see the *Christian Science Monitor*, November 8, 1979, p. 11, the *New York Times*, November 8, 1979, p. A18, and the *Washington Post*, November 8, 1979, p. 3.

14. For information see the *New York Times*, November 1, 1980, p. A11, the *Washington Post*, November 4, 1980, p. A15 and November 5, 1980, p. A19, and the *Christian Science Monitor*, November 7, 1980, p. 4.

15. The figures for the table come from a series of election day wrap-ups on referendums and initiatives by Austin Ranney that appeared in *Public Opinion*. In addition, data from odd-year elections and votes not held in November (for example, Proposition 13, the beginning of the tax revolt, was on the ballot in June 1978 and did not, therefore, figure in Ranney's wrap-up), I have searched the *New York Times*, the *Washington Post*, and the *Christian Science Monitor*. I am confident that I have found information on most, if not all, of the statewide ballot propositions dealing with taxing and spending limits. I may have missed a few which went unreported in those three papers, but I doubt that would change the results very much. Also, I have not included bonding propositions in the totals.

16. Cited in "Louisiana Changes Course and Accepts Tax Increase," the

New York Times, October 9, 1989, p. A8.

17. Both quotations were cited in the *Des Moines Register*, June 7, 1990, p. 3A.

18. For the Louisiana vote see the *New York Times*, October 9, 1989, p. A8. For the Pennsylvania vote see the *New York Times*, May 17, 1989, p. A20. For the others, see *Public Opinion*, January/February 1989, p. 17.

19. For the Cleveland vote see the *New York Times*, February 28, 1979, p. A3. For the Detroit vote see the *Washington Post*, June 24, 1981, p. A8. For the St. Louis and Kansas City votes see the *Christian Science Monitor*, November 9, 1989, p. 7. And for the New Orleans vote see the *New York Times*, January 19, 1987, p. 11.

20. The data comes from a survey done by the Gallup Organization in June of 1985 as reported in *Public Opinion*, March/April 1987, p. 26.

21. The *New York Times*, July 14, 1991, pp. A1, A6.

Chapter 5

1. Quoted in E.J. Dionne, Jr., "Analyzing the Electoral Vote: Does the GOP Have a "Lock"?" p. A1. According to Stuart Rothenberg in "A New Look at the Lock: How the Republicans Can Lose," this theory was first articulated by political analyst Horace Busby. Rothenberg also argued that the theory is incorrect. He said that the 1988 election will "turn on the candidates (their strengths and weaknesses), strategic campaign decisions, and events beyond the control of the campaigns. Compared with those factors, the lock is insignificant" (p. 54). I agree with Rothenberg's assessment, but I want to take the argument one step further. Rothenberg argued the Republicans cannot take victory for granted, that under the right circumstances, the Democrats can win. I want to show, in this chapter, that there is also an electoral basis from which we can elect a liberal Democratic President.

2. The quotation is taken from Robin Toner, "Democrats Urged to Veer to Center," p. 1.

3. In 1988 the total was 341. Add seven electoral votes from the South and four from the list of states the Republicans have carried in every election since 1964 but subtract two from the list of those states the Republicans have carried since 1968, for a total of 350.

4. The information on the state election outcomes is drawn from *Politics in America, The Almanac of American Politics*, and *Congressional Quarterly Weekly Reports*.

5. Measuring liberalism is not an easy thing to do, but ADA scores seem to be about as reasonable a measure as any. They do tend to reflect support for traditional American liberal policies. They run on a scale from 0 (extremely conservative) to 100 (a "perfect" liberal voting record). I consider any score over 85 to be clearly liberal, and any score over 75 to be reasonably liberal. Scores from 50 to 75 tend to reflect moderate voting records. Anything below 50 reflects a conservative voting pattern.

6. Maine is the only state in the nation which divides its electoral votes by congressional district. A candidate receives 1 electoral vote for each of the two districts he or she carries and a 2 electoral-vote bonus goes to the candidate who wins the entire state. Thus, theoretically, Maine's 4 electoral votes could be divided three to one, though this has never happened.

7. Michael Barone and Grant Ujifusa, *The Almanac of American Politics 1990*, p. 75.

Chapter 6

1. See, for example, John Petrocik, *Party Coalitions: Realignment and the Decline of the New Deal Party System*; Robert Axelrod, "Where the Votes Come From: An Analysis of Electoral Coalitions" and "Presidential Election Coalitions in 1984"; and the series by Paul Abramson, John Aldrich, and David Rohde, *Change and Continuity in the 1980 Elections, Change and Continuity in the 1984 Elections*, and *Change and Continuity in the 1988 Election*.

2. John Petrocik and Frederick Steeper, "The Political Landscape in 1988," p. 41.

3. See Edward Carmines and James Stimson, *Issue Evolution: Race and the Transformation of American Politics*, and Robert Huckfeldt and Carol Kohfeld, *Race and the Decline of Class in American Politics*.

4. Abramson, Aldrich, and Rohde, *Change and Continuity in the 1988 Elections*, p. 124.

5. Ibid., p. 125, and Petrocik and Steeper, "The Political Landscape in 1988," p. 41.

6. Ibid.

7. E.J. Dionne Jr., "Catholics and the Democrats: Estrangement but Not Desertion."

8. Henry Kenski, "The Catholic Voter in American Elections."

9. There is a large and rapidly growing scholarship on gender and voting. See, for example, Ethel Klein, *Gender Politics*; Sandra Baxter and Marjorie Lansing, *Women and Politics: The Visible Majority*; Pamela Conover, "Feminists and the Gender Gap"; Ethel Klein, "The Gender Gap: Different Issues, Different Answers"; and Robert Shapiro and Harpreet Mahajan, "Gender Differences in Policy Preferences: A Summary of Trends from the 1960s to the 1980s."

10. Abramson, Aldrich, and Rohde, *Change and Continuity in the 1988 Elections*, p. 126.

11. *The Gallup Report*, September 1988, p. 6.

12. See Everett Carll Ladd, "The 1988 Elections: Continuation of the Post-New Deal System," pp. 16–17.

13. See Ethel Klein, *Gender Politics*.

14. See Shapiro and Mahajan, "Gender Differences in Policy Preferences."

15. Herbert Weisberg, "The Demographics of a New Voting Gap: Marital Differences in American Voting," p. 335.

16. *The Gallup Report*, September 1988, p. 5, Abramson, Aldrich, and Rohde, *Change and Continuity in the 1988 Elections*, p. 124; and Ladd, "The 1988 Elections: Continuation of the Post-New Deal System."

17. Thomas Edsall, *The New Politics of Inequality*, and *Power and Money*.

18. Kevin Phillips, *The Politics of Rich and Poor*.

19. Petrocik and Steeper, "The Political Landscape in 1988," p. 42.

20. *The Gallup Report*, October 1989, p. 5, and October 1988, p. 34.

21. See Kenski, "The Catholic Voter in American National Elections"; Andrew Greeley, *American Catholics Since the Council*; and Kenneth Wald, *Religion and Politics in the United States*.

22. See, for example, Shapiro and Mahajan, "Gender Differences in Policy Preferences," or Sandra Baxter and Marjorie Lansing, *Women and Politics: The Visible Majority*.

23. See Robert Kuttner, *The Life of the Party: Democratic Prospects in 1988 and Beyond*. Kuttner argues that economic populism is the key to Democratic success. I agree with his view that economic issues are the key to holding the Democratic coalition together. However, I think he underestimates the potential for other issues (such as the environment and education) to help rebuild the Democratic Party, and I think he underestimates the need to deal more effectively with the implications of the perception that taxes are not fair.

24. The figures on education are from *The Gallup Report*, July 1986, p. 6. The environmental figures are from *The Gallup Poll Monthly*, April 1990, p. 12.

25. *The Gallup Poll Monthly*, January 1990, p. 12.

26. Kenski, "The Catholic Voter in American Elections," p. 18.

27. *The Gallup Poll Monthly*, February 1990, p. 12.

28. Quoted in Steve Lilienthel, "Stan Greenberg: Polling for Pols," p. 5.

29. David Sears and Jack Citrin, *Tax Revolt: Something for Nothing in California*, p. 185.

30. *The Gallup Poll Monthly*, December 1989, p. 22 and June 1991, p. 32, and *The Gallup Report*, July 1988, p. 17.

31. The story was aired on September 26, 1991. It used a method of following with hidden cameras a black man and a white man into stores and on visits to prospective employers and prospective landlords to look for differences in treatment. The results were consistent and stark. In every place they went, the white man was treated much better than the black man. Store clerks ignored the black man (or watched him suspiciously) while they offered help to the white man. An apartment was "already taken" when the black man asked about it, but moments later it was available to the white man. Jobs followed a similar pattern of "being filled" when the applicant was black. As Walter Goodman noted in his review of the program in the *New York Times*, the only note for optimism was the strong denials of racial prejudice on the part of those individuals confronted by ABC News. For Goodman's review see "Looking Racism in the Face in St. Louis," p. C22.

32 For example, when asked in 1988 if they supported the establishment of an independent Palestinian nation, 38 percent of whites said they did compared

with 34 percent of blacks. Similarly, when asked if the Israeli handling of the Intifada had made them less supportive of Israel, 31 percent of whites said it had, but only 22 percent of blacks said so. On the other hand, when asked if they generally supported Israel, the Palestinian Arabs, or neither, whites responded: 45 percent, Israel; 19 percent, Palestinian Arabs; and 20 percent, neither. Blacks responded 35 percent, Israel; 20 percent, Palestinian Arabs; and 26 percent, neither. See *The Gallup Report*, March 1988, p. 14 and May 1988, p. 22.

33. *The Gallup Report*, October 1988, p. 34.

34. *The Gallup Poll Monthly*, April 1990, p. 4.

35. *The Gallup Report*, March/April 1989, p. 3. and August 1988, p. 3.

36. See Norman Ornstein, Andrew Kohut, and Larry McCarthy, *The People, The Press and Politics.*

37. Ibid., pp. 13–17.

38. Ibid., p. 95.

39. Ibid., p. 96.

40. Ibid., pp. 77–78.

41. Ibid., p. 78.

Chapter 7

1. Andrew Kohut and Norman Ornstein, "Constructing a Winning Coalition," p. 41.

2. Paul Abramson, John Aldrich, and David Rohde, *Change and Continuity in the 1988 Elections*, pp. 124–125.

3. Martin Wattenberg, "From a Partisan to a Candidate-centered Electorate," p. 162.

4. Ibid., p. 163.

5. Larry Sabato, *The Party's Just Begun*, p. 161.

6. Ibid., p. 155.

7. Abramson, Aldrich, and Rohde, *Change and Continuity in the 1988 Elections*, p. 110.

8. *The Gallup Report*, March/April 1989, p. 24.

9. Cited in *Public Opinion*, March/April 1987, p. 26.

10. See, for example, George Nash, *The Conservative Intellectual Movement in America Since 1945*, or Kenneth Dolbeare and Linda Medcalf, *American Ideologies Today.*

11. *The Gallup Report*, January 1986, p. 13.

12. *The Gallup Report*, July 1988, p. 16.

13. Reported in Robin Toner, "The Uproar over What America Owes Its First Allegiance To," p. 1.

14. Abramson, Aldrich, and Rohde, *Change and Continuity in the 1988 Elections*, p. 191.

15. Ibid., p. 193.

16. *The Gallup Poll Monthly*, April 1990, p. 4.

17. *Webster v. Reproductive Health Services, 1989*.

18. Wattenberg, "From a Partisan to a Candidate-centered Electorate," p. 168.

19. Cited in *Public Opinion*, March/April 1987, p. 24.

20. *The Gallup Poll Monthly*, April 1990, p. 11.

21. Norman Ornstein, Andrew Kohut, and Larry McCarthy, *The People, The Press, and Politics*, pp. 13–17.

22. Ibid., p. 96.

Chapter 8

1. See Daniel Patrick Moynihan, *Maximum Feasible Misunderstanding*.

2. See Robert Kuttner, *The Life of the Party*, and Kevin Phillips, *The Politics of Rich and Poor*.

3. Kuttner, *The Life of the Party*, p. 230.

4. Kuttner, *The Life of the Party*, pp. 224–241. The quotation appears on p. 231.

5. Quoted in Kuttner, *The Life of the Party*, p. 10.

6. Just as the public likes liberal policies but does not think very favorably of liberals, it likes feminist policies but does not like feminists (or "women's libbers"). I have taught a class on "women and politics" for the past six years, and I am always struck by the number of students who tell me that they "are not feminists" on the first day of class and then, over the course of the semester, show support for just about all feminist principles and policies. Progressive Democrats need to show their support for feminist policies and principles while working to redefine people's views of what a "feminist" is.

Chapter 9

1. Walter Dean Burnham, *Critical Elections and the Mainsprings of American Politics*, p. 133.

2. See, for example, Austin Ranney, *Curing the Mischiefs of Faction*, or Larry Sabato, *The Party's Just Begun*.

3. Sabato, *The Party's Just Begun*, p. 133.

4. E.E. Schattschneider, *The Semisovereign People*, p. 35.

5. Sabato, *The Party's Just Begun*, pp. 179–183.

6. Harry Boyte, *CommonWealth*.

7. See, for example, Richard Hall and Harry Wayman, "Buying Time: Moneyed Interests and the Mobilization of Bias in Congressional Committees"; John Owens, "The Impact of Campaign Contributions on Legislative Outcomes in Congress: Evidence from a House Committee"; John Wright, "PACs, Contributions, and Roll Calls: An Organizational Perspective"; Benjamin Ginsberg and John Green, "The Best Congress Money Can Buy: Contributions and Congressional Behavior"; and Frank Sorauf, *Money in American Elections*.

8. Frances Fox Piven and Richard Cloward, *Why Americans Don't Vote*, especially Chapter 4.

9. Piven and Cloward, *Why Americans Don't Vote*, Chapter 7.

10. See Thomas Edsall, *The New Politics of Inequality*, and Robert Kuttner, *The Life of the Party*.

11. See Kuttner, *The Life of the Party*, Chapter 2.

12. See R. Kenneth Godwin, *One Billion Dollars of Influence*.

13. Gary Jacobson, *The Politics of Congressional Elections*, Chapter 4.

14. All spending figures come from Michael Barone and Grant Ujifusa, *The Almanac of American Politics 1990*. Adams was outspent 3.2 million dollars to 1.9 million dollars, Conrad was outspent 2.2 million dollars to 900,000 dollars, Fowler was outspent 5.1 million dollars to 2.7 million dollars, and Shelby was outspent 4.6 million dollars to 2.2 million dollars.

15. Charles Babcock, "Money Isn't Everything," p. 15.

Bibliography

Abramson, Paul, Aldrich, John, and Rohde, David. *Change and Continuity in the 1980 Elections.* Washington, DC: CQ Press, 1982.

———. *Change and Continuity in the 1984 ElectionS.* Washington, DC: CQ Press, 1986.

———. *Change and Continuity in the 1988 ElectionS.* Washington, DC: CQ Press, 1990.

Adams, William. "Recent Fables about Ronald Reagan." *Public Opinion* 7 (October/November 1984): 6–9.

Axelrod, Robert. "Where the Votes Come From: An Analysis of Electoral Coalitions." *American Political Science Review* 66 (1972): 11–20.

———. "Presidential Election Coalitions in 1984." *American Political Science Review* 80 (1986): 281–284.

Babcock, Charles. "Money Isn't Everything." *The Washington Post National Weekly Edition* (November 12–18, 1990): 15.

Barone, Michael and Ujifusa, Grant. *The Almanac of American Politics 1990.* Washington, DC: The National Journal, 1989.

Baxter, Sandra and Lansing, Marjorie. *Women and Politics: The Visible Majority.* Revised edition. Ann Arbor: University of Michigan Press, 1983.

Boyte, Harry. *CommonWealth.* New York: Free Press, 1989.

Brady, Henry, and Sniderman, Paul. "Attitude Attribution: A Group Basis for Political Reasoning." *American Political Science Review* 25 (1985): 1061–1078.

Burnham, Walter Dean. *Critical Elections and the Mainsprings of American Politics.* New York: W.W. Norton, 1970.

Carmines, Edward, and Stimson, James. *Issue Evolution: Race and the Transformation of American Politics.* Princeton: Princeton University Press, 1989.

Ceaser, James. "The Reagan Presidency and American Public Opinion." In *The Reagan Legacy,* ed. Charles O. Jones, pp. 172–210. Chatham, N.J.: Chatham House, 1988.

Conover, Pamela. "Feminists and the Gender Gap." *Journal of Politics* 50 (1988): 985–1010.

Conover, Pamela, and Feldman, Stanley. "The Origins and Meaning of Liberal/Conservative Self-Identifications." *American Journal of Political Science* 79 (1981): 1061–1078.

DeStafano, Linda, and Colasanto, Diane. "Unlike 1975, Today Most Americans Think Men Have It Better." *The Gallup Poll Monthly* (February 1990): 25–36.

Dionne, Jr., E.J. "Analyzing the Electoral Vote: Does the GOP Have a "Lock"?" The *New York Times* (October 12, 1988): A1.

———. "Catholics and the Democrats: Estrangement but Not Desertion." In *Party Coalitions in the 1980s*, ed. Seymour M. Lipset. San Francisco: Institute for Contemporary Studies, 1981.

Doble, John, and Melvile, Keith. "The Public's Social Welfare Mandate," *Public Opinion* 11 (January/February 1989): 48–51.

Dolbeare, Kenneth and Medcalf, Linda. *American Ideologies Today*. New York: Random House, 1988.

Edelman, Murray. *Constructing the Political Spectacle*. Chicago: University of Chicago Press, 1988.

———. *The Symbolic Uses of Politics*. Urbana: University of Illinois Press, 1964.

Edsall, Thomas. *The New Politics of Inequality*. New York: W.W. Norton, 1984.

———. *Power and Money*. New York: W.W. Norton, 1988.

Elshtain, Jean Bethke. "Issues and Themes in the 1988 Campaign." In *The Elections of 1988*, ed. Michael Nelson, pp. 111–126. Washington, DC: CQ Press, 1989.

Epstein, Edward. *News from Nowhere*. New York: Random House, 1973.

Farah, Barbara, and Klein, Ethel. "Public Opinion Trends." In *The Election of 1988*, ed. Gerald Pomper et al., pp. 103–128. Chatham, NJ: Chatham House, 1989.

Ferguson, Thomas, and Rogers, Joel. *Right Turn: The 1984 Election and the Future of American Politics*. New York: Hill and Wang, 1986.

Fiorina, Morris. *Retrospective Voting in American National Elections*. New Haven: Yale University Press, 1981.

Frankovic, Kathleen. "Public Opinion Trends." In *The Election of 1980*, ed. Gerald Pomper, et al., pp. 97–118. Chatham, NJ: Chatham House, 1981.

Free, Lloyd and Cantril, Hadley. *The Political Beliefs of Americans*. New York: Simon and Schuster, 1968.

Ginsberg, Benjamin, and Green, John. "The Best Congress Money Can Buy: Contributions and Congressional Behavior." In *Do Elections Matter?*, ed. Benjamin Ginsberg and Alan Stone, pp. 75–89. Armonk, NY: M.E. Sharpe,1986.

Godwin, R. Kenneth. *One Billion Dollars of Influence*. Chatham, N.J.: Chatham House, 1988.

Goodman, Walter. "Looking Racism in the Face in St. Louis." The *New York Times* (September 26, 1991): C22.

Graber, Doris. *Mass Media and American Politics*. Washington, D.C.: Congressional Quarterly, 1986.

Greeley, Andrew. *American Catholics Since the Council.* Chicago: Thomas More, 1985.

Greenhouse, Linda. "Despite Support, A Child Care Bill Fails to Emerge." The *New York Times* (June 6, 1988): A14.

Hall, Richard, and Wayman, Harry. "Buying Time: Moneyed Interests and the Mobilization of Bias in Congressional Committees." *American Political Science Review* 84 (1990):797–820.

Huckfeldt, Robert, and Kohfeld, Carol. *Race and the Decline of Class in American Politics.* Urbana: University of Illinois Press, 1989.

Jacobson, Gary, *The Politics of Congressional Elections.* 2d ed. Boston: Little, Brown, 1987.

Keeter, Scott. "Public Opinion in 1984." In *The Election of 1984,* ed. Gerald Pomper et al., pp. 91–111. Chatham, NJ: Chatham House, 1985.

Kenski, Henry. "The Catholic Voter in American Elections." *Election Politics* 5 (Spring 1988): 16–23.

Klein, Ethel. "The Gender Gap: Different Issues, Different Answers." *The Brookings Review* 3 (1985): 33–37.

———. *Gender Politics.* Cambridge: Harvard University Press, 1984.

Knight, Kathleen. "Ideological Identification and the Content of the Ideological Agenda, 1960–1980." A paper presented at the Annual Meeting of the American Political Science Association, Washington, DC, 1984.

Kohut, Andrew, and Hugick, Larry. "Taxes and Federal Programs: Public Supports Higher Taxes for Domestic Programs: Education, Drug War Lead The List." *The Gallup Report* (October 1989): 4–10.

Kohut, Andrew and Ornstein, Norman. "Constructing a Winning Coalition." *Public Opinion* 10 (November/December 1987): 41–44.

Kraus, Sidney, and Davis, Dennis. *The Effects of Mass Communication on Political Behavior.* University Park: Pennsylvania State University Press, 1978.

Kuttner, Robert. *The Life of the Party: Democratic Prospects in 1988 and Beyond.* New York: Penguin Books, 1988.

Ladd, Everett Carll, "Abortion: Trouble for Both Parties." *Public Opinion* 12 (May/June 1989): 3–8.

———. "The 1988 Elections: Continuation of the Post-New Deal System." *Political Science Quarterly* 104 (1989): 1–18.

Lake, Celinda, and Greenberg, Stanley. "What's Left for Liberalism." *Public Opinion* 12 (March/April 1989): 4–7.

Lewin, Tamar. "Daycare Becomes a Growing Burden." The *New York Times* (June 5, 1988): A22.

Lilienthel, Steve. "Stan Greenberg: Polling for Pols." *In These Times* (September 25, 1990): 5.

Lowi, Theodore. "An Aligning Election: A Presidential Plebiscite." In *The Elections of 1984.,* ed. Michael Nelson, pp. 277–302. Washington, DC: CQ Press, 1985.

Moynihan, Daniel Patrick. *Maximum Feasible Misunderstanding.* New York: The Free Press, 1969.

Nash, George. *The Conservative Intellectual Movement in America Since 1945*. New York: Basic Books, 1976.

Newport, Frank. "Tax Reform Fails to Achieve its Goals." *The Gallup Poll Monthly* (March 1990): 6–10.

Nimmo, Dan, and Coombs, James. *Mediated Political Realities*. 2d ed. New York: Longman, 1990.

Ornstein, Norman, Kohut, Andrew, and McCarthy, Larry. *The People, The Press and Politics*. Reading, MA: Addison-Wesley, 1988.

Ostrom, Jr., Charles and Simon, Dennis. "The Man in the Teflon Suit?" *Public Opinion Quarterly* 53 (1989): 353–387.

Owens, John. "The Impact of Campaign Contributions on Legislative Outcomes in Congress: Evidence from a House Committee." *Political Studies* 34 (1986): 285–295.

Page, Benjamin. *Choices and Echoes in Presidential Elections*. Chicago: University of Chicago Press, 1978.

Petrocik, John. *Party Coalitions: Realignment and the Decline of the New Deal Party System*. Chicago: University of Chicago Press, 1980.

Petrocik, John and Steeper, Frederick. "The Political Landscape in 1988." *Public Opinion* 10 (September/October 1987): 41–44.

Phillips, Kevin. *The Politics of Rich and Poor*. New York: Random House, 1990.

Piven, Frances Fox, and Cloward, Richard. *Why Americans Don't Vote*. New York: Pantheon Books, 1988.

Ranney, Austin. *Channels of Power*. New York: American Enterprise Institute, 1983.

———. *Curing the Mischiefs of Faction*. Berkeley: University of California Press, 1975.

Rothenberg, Stuart. "A New Look at the Lock: How the Republicans Can Lose." *Public Opinion* 10 (March/April 1988): 41–42, 54.

Sabato, Larry. *The Party's Just Begun*. Glenview, IL: Scott, Foresman, 1988.

Sanders, Arthur. "Ideological Symbols." *American Politics Quarterly* 17 (1989): 227–255.

———. *Making Sense of Politics*. Ames, IA: Iowa State University Press, 1990.

———. "Making Sense of Politics." A paper presented at the Annual Meeting of the American Political Science Association, Washington, DC, 1991.

———. "The Meaning of Liberalism and Conservatism." *Polity* 19 (1986): 123–135.

———. "Rationality, Self-Interest, and Public Attitudes on Public Spending." *Social Science Quarterly* 69 (1988): 311–324.

Sanders, Arthur, and Wagner, Kenneth. "The Myth of Charisma in American Politics." *Social Policy* 18 (Winter 1988): 57–61.

Schattschneider, E.E. *The Semisovereign People* . New York: Holt, Rinehart and Winston, 1960.

Schneider, William. "Abortion: Trouble for the GOP." *Public Opinion* 12 (May/June 1989): 1, 59–60

————. "The November 4 Vote for President: What Did It Mean?" In *The American Elections of 1980*, ed. Austin Ranney, pp. 212–262. Washington, DC: American Enterprise Institute, 1981.

Sears, David, and Citrin, Jack. *Tax Revolt*. Enlarged edition. Cambridge, MA: Harvard University Press, 1985.

Shapiro, Robert, and Mahajan, Harpreet. "Gender Differences in Policy Preferences: A Summary of Trends from the 1960s to the 1980s." *Public Opinion Quarterly* 50 (1986): 42–61.

Sigelman, Lee and Knight, Kathleen. "Expectation/Disillusion and Presidential Popularity: The Reagan Experience." *Public Opinion Quarterly* 49 (1985): 209–213.

Smith, Jeffrey. *American Presidential Elections: Trust and the Rational Voter*. Westport, CT: Praeger, 1980.

Sorauf, Frank. *Money in American Elections*. Glenview, IL: Scott, Foresman, 1988.

Toner, Robin. "Democrats Urged to Veer to Center." The *New York Times* (November 14, 1989): A1.

————. "Dukakis Aides Acknowledge Bush Outmaneuvered Them." The *New York Times* (November 12, 1988): A1, A8.

————. "Poll Finds Postwar Glow Dimmed by the Economy." The *New York Times* (March 8, 1991): A11.

————. "The Uproar over What America Owes Its First Allegiance To." The *New York Times* (July 2, 1989, section 4): 1.

Wald, Kenneth D. *Religion and Politics in the United States*. New York: St. Martin's Press, 1987.

Wattenberg, Martin. "From a Partisan to a Candidate-centered Electorate." In *The New American Political System.*. Second Version, ed. Anthony King. Washington, DC: American Enterprise Institute, 1990.

Weisberg, Herbert. "The Demographics of a New Voting Gap: Marital Differences in American Voting." *Public Opinion Quarterly* 51 (1987): 335–343.

Weisman, Steven. "Can the Magic Prevail?" The *New York Times Magazine* (April 29, 1984): 38–56.

Wright, John. "PACs, Contributions, and Roll Calls: An Organizational Perspective." *American Political Science Review* 79 (1985): 400–414.

Yeric, Jerry, and Todd, John. *Public Opinion: The Visible Politics*. 2d ed. Itasca, IL: F.E. Peacock, 1989.

Index

About the Author

Arthur Sanders is Assistant Professor of Political Science at Drake University in Des Moines, Iowa. He is the author of *Making Sense of Politics*. He also has written a number of articles about American public opinion and electoral politics for journals such as *Western Political Quarterly, American Politics Quarterly, Social Science Quarterly, Social Policy,* and *Election Politics*.